Other Books by Patrick Morley

P9-CDY-199

Patrick Morley

Is Christianity for You?
Copyright © 2013 by Patrick M. Morley
ISBN: 978-0-9679122-9-5

Cover design by Kevin McMillan
Layout and interior design by Cathleen Kwas

Printed in the United States of America

Dedication

To my wife, Patsy,
who introduced me to the Christian faith.

Contents

Chapter 1

"Why Am I Still So Restless?"

One summer in Oxford, England, I was walking between two buildings that amplified sound like an old European cathedral. The superior acoustics had not gone unnoticed by a street musician who was strumming his guitar and singing for pocket change. Chills went up and down my spine as his lyrics reverberated off the buildings:

So this is what it feels like to be lonely,
So this is what it feels like to be small,
So this is what it feels like to realize,
My work doesn't matter at all.

His words capture the feelings of someone who has run their experiment—perhaps successfully, perhaps not—but still feels the weight of life's futility.

The Feeling of Futility

Sometimes we're on top of the mountain. But sometimes we feel like the mountain is on top of us. We all know we're going to experience both good times and bad times. Every life is a strange mixture of joy and sadness, of good and evil.

There is, however, a *third force* at work in the world that's neither good nor evil. It's futility—those things that seem useless, meaningless, or like a big waste. Many things happen to us that are not evil per se, yet leave us wondering, *What was that all about?*

If you had a flat tire, ran out of gas, got stuck in a two-hour traffic delay, or lost your best customer to a competitor, you would not say, "This is evil." Those are disappointments, not evil things—but they do seem pretty pointless.

Other examples are more serious. Here are some real comments from people I've met:

> A young man struggling with futility finally summarized it like this: "If I had known how empty I would end up feeling, I wouldn't have done it this way."

> At the age of thirty-one, Susan had twenty-four people reporting to her. Yet she said, "I'm just not happy." She found it hard to see how her work was important, but her responsibilities forced her to fake it. Often, the dilemma is

not so much that we are unhappy, but that we must pretend we are happy.

For others of us, futility means our lives are falling apart. Warren, at an age when most men are playing with grandchildren, told me he didn't know where his ex-wife lived, and his son, much to Warren's disappointment, couldn't keep a job.

A middle-aged woman said, "After all I've been through, after surviving several major crises, after all the obstacles I've overcome, after all the work I've put into this life, after getting the spouse that I wanted, after getting the children that I assumed would bring me joy, after all I've achieved, after all of this, why am I still so restless?"

No one is immune.

Ironically, many of us feel like our lives are futile not because we didn't get what we wanted, but because we did. After a seminar I taught, Brian said, "Two weeks ago I received an award for being the top salesman in my company. But it just doesn't satisfy. There is no purpose. It didn't mean anything. What's the use?" There were tears in his eyes.

Worldly success has eluded a friend of mine for his entire life. He is as depressed that he didn't achieve worldly success as I was when I did. We had two opposite circumstantial results—yet the same depressive outcome.

> *Many of us feel like our lives are futile not because we didn't get what we wanted, but because we did.*

Both success and failure can leave us feeling empty. We can work hard and achieve a goal that leaves us wondering, *What's the point?* Or on another occasion, we can fail to achieve a goal that leaves us thinking, *Why bother?*

Futility comes when life doesn't turn out like you planned—not because some evil befell you, but simply because life is so messy. That's why most us will spend a lot more time struggling against futility than against evil.

Christianity claims to solve a number of problems that people have. But I think the most sharply "felt" problem it remedies is the feeling that life is pointless.

Unexpected Questions

Whether you grew up in a religious home or not, sooner or later all of us end up wrestling with a handful of unexpected, spiritually-charged questions:

- Why am I still so restless?
- Why do I feel empty?
- Why do I feel lonely?
- Why do I keep repeating the same mistakes?
- Why do I feel like my life lacks purpose?
- Will anything I do ever make a difference?
- Does my life matter?
- Does anybody really care?
- What happens when I die?
- Where can I go for relief?

Now for some good news. Christianity has answers for these questions.

The Purpose of This Book

One of my seminary professors told a story about a man out for a hike on a cold winter day. He came to a river that appeared to be frozen over. But since he was unfamiliar with the area, he didn't know how thick the ice was. Naturally, he was afraid that if he walked out he might fall through. So he got down on his stomach and slowly began to inch his way out onto the ice.

When he had crawled near the middle of the river, the air began to tremble as he heard a rumbling sound draw closer and closer. Suddenly a wagon with four horses at a full gallop shot over the crest of the riverbank, thundered across the river, and then disappeared over the ridge on the other side. You can imagine how foolish he felt.

A lot of genuine, sincere people have honest doubts and questions about Christianity.

It's difficult to trust something we don't know much about, isn't it? The man lying on the ice had difficulty trusting the ice because he didn't know much about the river.

But it isn't odd he felt that way. What would have been odd is if he had walked up to an unfamiliar frozen river and confidently stepped out on it.

Frankly, a lot of people feel this same lack of confidence about what they believe— and they don't like it one bit. It's completely understandable that a lot of genuine, sincere people have honest doubts and questions about Christianity. You may be one of them.

The purpose of this book is to help you answer the questions, "Is Christianity for me?" and "Can I examine Christianity rationally and determine whether it is a belief system that is true?" I believe the answer to both of these questions is "Yes."

You will find nothing new or novel in these pages. Everything I'll say comes directly out of the tradition of classic, historic, orthodox Christianity. It is intended to give you the feeling of a solid mass across which you can safely walk—not thin ice.

The Plan

For the most part, I've found that it's more important to explain the Christian faith than defend it, since more people are misinformed about Christianity than oppose it.

So how will we proceed?

To answer life's most challenging questions, we all progress—and sometimes regress—through a series of four belief systems: *secular, moral, religious*, and *Christian*. So whether you are a seeker or a skeptic, an agnostic or an atheist, Part One will help you understand these four major belief systems and assess where you are today.

In Part Two, we'll answer some of the most common questions and objections about Christianity, such as:

- Is the idea of God logical?

- Shouldn't science rule over theology?

- If God is good, why is there so much suffering?

- How can you stake your entire life on believing the Bible is true?

- Is it "reasonable" to believe in the Christian faith?

Finally, in Part Three, I'll show you the historic, orthodox way of making Christianity your own, and give you a few suggestions for how to grow in your Christian faith.

> *It's more important to explain the Christian faith than defend it, since more people are misinformed about Christianity than oppose it.*

I'm convinced that what you'll read in these pages is the truth that can help you become the person God created you to be. God loves you very much and wants to fill your life with meaning, hope, peace, and purpose.

Part One.

Four Belief Systems

Chapter 2

What Do You Believe?

"Your system is perfectly designed to produce the result you are getting."

No one who ends up feeling empty inside would have let it happen if they had seen it coming. So how does it happen?

In the world of business, there is a very helpful idea: "Your system is perfectly designed to produce the result you are getting."

For example, if you manufacture cars and every third car that rolls off the assembly line is missing a front right fender, your system is perfectly designed to produce that result.

Or, if you sell insurance and the person in the office next to you consistently sells twice as much as you, his or her system is perfectly designed to produce that result. Unfortunately, your system is perfectly designed to sell the lesser amount.

There are many types of systems, such as banking systems, prison systems, civil defense systems, transportation systems, data processing systems, national defense systems, heating and air conditioning systems, digestive systems, and circulatory systems.

Systems provide order, efficiency, and predictable results. But once the wrong system is designed, the wrong result is inevitable.

There are also *belief* systems. A good synonym for belief system is *worldview*. A belief system, or worldview, is the collection of ideas we believe about the most important issues in life—ultimate reality, knowledge, ethics, humankind, and God.[1]

If you are feeling puny about life—maybe you have a deep-seated emptiness or feel like what you do is meaningless—it means you have a "systems" problem. Your belief system is perfectly designed to produce the result you are getting—even though it's not what you want.

Here's the problem: if the belief system you build doesn't work, you probably won't know it for ten or twenty years. By then the damage is done, and you will have given the best years of your life to a belief system that failed you.

However, at that point, most of us can't afford to "drop out" or make sweeping

---

1. Ron Nash, *Worldviews in Conflict* (Grand Rapids: Zondervan, 1992), 19-30.

changes because we're up to our necks in
a mind-numbing array of debts, duties, and
obligations.

For example, one day I asked a friend,
"How are you doing?"

He said, "Friday night I got back into my
office at 6:00 p.m. I had 148 emails and 45
voicemails. I couldn't go home until I at least
returned the priority voicemails. Now, what
was your question?"

Four Belief Systems

In books about meaning and purpose, you
see a pattern of four different belief systems—what I call *secular, moral, religious,* and
Christian. These systems
have been given various
names like "phases of
the soul," the "strands"
or "stages" of religion,
worldviews, life stages,
spheres, or stages along
life's way. The following
few paragraphs may be a little bit of heavy
reading, but I want you to see for yourself
that these ideas have been discussed by
many different thinkers and writers. In other
words, I'm saying nothing new.

> *These belief systems
> are trying to solve
> the same problems
> in different ways.*

Søren Kierkegaard, the Christian writer many also consider the father of existentialism, called his systems the *aesthetic, ethical,* and *religious* spheres, and then further divided his religious sphere into *religiousness A* for what all religions have in common, and *religiousness B* for true Christianity.

C. S. Lewis in *The Problem of Pain* identified three strands or elements in all developed religions, and a fourth strand in Christianity. He called the first strand the experience of the *numinous* (which I talk more about in Chapter 3). The second is the consciousness of a *moral law*. The third strand is to allow the numinous power we worship to become the *guardian* of our morality. And the fourth strand is *Christianity*, which is different because it is based on an historical event.

The apostle Paul, using categories he writes about in the Bible, calls his stages the *flesh,* the *law,* and the *Spirit.* When referring to the "law," Paul distinguished between God's moral law (let's call this Law I) and the no-longer-in-effect religious law of the Old Covenant (Law II).

Take a look at these systems compared to each other:

	Secular ➡	Moral ➡	Religious ➡	Christian
Kierkegaard	Aesthetic	Ethical	Religious A	Religious B
Lewis	Nonbeliever	Moral Law	Numinous	Christianity
Apostle Paul	Flesh	Law I	Law II	Spirit

Figure 1. Four Belief Systems

Whatever we call them, it's important to note that these four belief systems are not trying to solve *different* problems. They are actually trying to solve the *same* problems in different ways. We'll take a closer look at all four of these in the next two chapters, but first, let's understand why most belief systems break down.

A Common Story

Consider a representative couple, James and Jenny. They married shortly after they finished their education. They dreamed of becoming affluent enough to meet their needs and satisfy their wants, so they adopted a *secular belief system*. They both found promising work and started climbing the ladders. After five years, however, they had lived enough and seen enough things to realize that their greatest joy wasn't making money, but actually helping people.

They matured from a *secular belief system* into a *moral belief system*. Their credo became, "Try to be a better person and love others."

Another three years peeled off the calendar, and even though they could both say, "I tried to do the right thing by every person I met," they still experienced a vacuum in their souls. One day as they reviewed their lives "so far" they recognized there was still a spiritual void.

In the following weeks they started attending a neighborhood church. They found one that emphasized the values they wanted to carry forward into their religion—a gospel of love and social responsibility. They had always thought these values were important, so they embraced a *religious belief system* of love and good deeds.

The next five years flew by, until one day they asked each other, "Why are we still so restless?" As they talked it through, they realized there were elements of truth in each belief system they had tried, but somehow they still weren't satisfied. They felt like they had been robbed of some of the best years of their lives. Their whole paradigm was breaking up, but they didn't understand why.

How can this all too common experience be explained?

Why Belief Systems Break Down

Thomas Kuhn, author of *The Structure of Scientific Revolutions*, is the guru of why systems come and go. In the scientific world, someone develops a system, or paradigm, to explain how some part of the world works. After a while, though, anomalies or deviations start to appear. At first, a few of these can be explained—or explained away. However, with the passage of time the anomalies keep adding up and become increasingly difficult to fit into the existing system. Eventually the whole system comes under suspicion.

Then someone proposes a new system (or theory) that resolves the problems of the existing system. Because the solution seems to be good, it is enthusiastically embraced, until after a while it, too, has anomalies that begin to appear. And so the cycle repeats. For example, for two hundred years Newton's ideas about physics were considered the best approximation of what we saw in nature. But as scientists were able to measure more things with ever-increasing accuracy, more and more anomalies were observed. So along came Einstein with a new paradigm that still reigns today.

The same progression happens with our personal belief systems. All belief systems contain traces of truth. Obviously, none of us would adopt a belief system unless we honestly thought it addressed the real problems we're trying to solve. As one of my professors was fond of saying, "It takes a lot of truth to float an error."

> We have to make many of our most important decisions at an age when we are least prepared to make them wisely.

Nevertheless, there's a progression as beliefs break down and are replaced. Our worldviews morph and build on each other as we add to our life experiences, as suggested by the arrows in Figure 1. Since every system has some good to it, it's only natural that after investing five, ten, or twenty years believing a worldview, that you will want to carry over the remaining kernels of good and truth into your new system.

Of course, you may skip one or more phases (and save yourself a lot of heartache). Or you can also lapse and fall backward, for example, from a religious belief system into a secular one.

Why do our early belief systems not work out? Unfortunately, we have to make many of our most important decisions at an age when we are least prepared to make them wisely. It can then take many years to see the flaws in what we believed. But when we do come to our senses, we want to make a change.

That's exactly what happened to Solomon, the son of King David.

Solomon's Project

Among the talented men of history, few stand in Solomon's league. He was the richest, most powerful, most respected leader of his era. He was able to have whatever he wanted, whenever he wanted it. He lived at a level of luxury unparalleled in his day.

Solomon pursued every possible earthly avenue to find meaning and happiness. It became his passionate mission. He wrote, "I wanted to see what was worthwhile for men to do under heaven during the few days of their lives" (Ecclesiastes 2:3). He was interested in the question, "What does a man gain for all his toil?" (Ecclesiastes 2:22).

> *If your belief system isn't working, don't pretend it is.*

Because of his virtually unlimited resources, Solomon had opportunities few of us will ever have. He amassed a formidable résumé in business, education, literary achievements, science, real estate developments, military power, and wealth accumulation. He also indulged his senses with a wide array of worldly pleasures.

But after decades of achievement Solomon still found happiness elusive. Every gift was an empty box. He wrote these stirring words:

> I denied myself nothing my eyes desired;
> I refused my heart no pleasure.
> My heart took delight in all my work, and this was the reward for all my labor.
> Yet when I surveyed all that my hands had done and what I had toiled to achieve, everything was meaningless, a chasing after the wind; nothing was gained under the sun....
> So I hated life...(Ecclesiastes 2:10–11, 17)

Why did Solomon's belief system fail him? Solomon's system broke down because, even after getting everything he ever wanted, he still felt empty inside. That doesn't have to happen to you.

If your belief system isn't working, don't pretend it is. Obviously, any person's first choice would be to not make a mistake at all, but if you have, at least don't pretend you haven't. As the saying goes, no matter how far you have traveled down a wrong road, the only solution is to turn back and find a different way.

Next, let's develop a better understanding of these four belief systems.

Chapter 3

Secular, Moral, and Religious Belief Systems

Writer C. S. Lewis said:

Every age has its own outlook.... All contemporary writers share to some extent the contemporary outlook—even those, like myself, who seem most opposed to it. Nothing strikes me more when I read the controversies of past ages than the fact that both sides were usually assuming without question a good deal which we should now absolutely deny. They thought that they were as completely opposed as two sides could be, but in fact they were all the time secretly united—united *with* each other and *against* earlier and later ages—by a great mass of common assumptions.[2]

---

2. C. S. Lewis, *God in the Dock* (Grand Rapids: Eerdmans, 1970), 202.

Lewis's point is true because we all have many assumptions and fundamental beliefs that we rarely think about. Each belief system has its own outlook—a mass of common assumptions that unite against other world-views. Which one of the following belief systems best describes your outlook now?

A Secular Belief System

The first season of life is often used to find out who we are—our *identity*—and what our lives are about—our *purpose*. One day I asked a college student who was about to graduate, "What's your next step?"

> *Even if you can get all you want in this world, it will not be enough to make you happy.*

"Law school," he answered.

"So, then, you're going to change the world!"

"No," he said, "I'm going to make some money."

For most of us, our starter worldview—our default system, so-to-speak—is a *secular belief system* that glorifies at least one of the four Bs: beauty, brains, bucks, and brawn. The highest value of this belief system is captured in the concept of the ancient Greek philosopher Epicurus: Maximize pleasure and minimize pain.

Most secular people are decent human beings trying to raise families, be good neighbors, show some civic pride, earn a living, and enjoy a few pleasures. But by definition, the secular worldview does not seek meaning beyond the physical realm. These people are not yet asking many questions for which Christianity is the answer. They still think, *Money will solve my problems and success will make me happy.*

Here's the catch: Even if you can get all you want in this world, it will not be enough to make you happy.

Five, ten, or twenty adult years of living by a secular system leaves most people weary, confused, and bored. As former tennis superstar Andre Agassi said, "Without the cake, the icing sucks."

We start looking for diversions to anesthetize the pain. Christian philosopher and mathematician Blaise Pascal said, "They spend all day chasing a hare that they would not have wanted to buy."[3]

After pondering the human condition, the famously secular Frenchman Jean-Paul Sartre concluded there was no God and that life was hopeless. He said, "Man is an empty bubble with nothing at the center.

---

3. Blaise Pascal, *Pensées*, #136 (London: Penguin Books, 1966), 68.

Man commits himself, draws his portrait, and that's all there is. Life is a useless passion."[4]

Indeed, the nature of life can be tragic and futile. However, man is not empty of meaning. Christian thinker Francis Schaeffer explained it this way:

> The Bible teaches that, though man is lost, he is not nothing. Man is lost because he is separated from God, his true reference point, by true moral guilt. But he will never be nothing. There lies the horror of his lostness. For man to be lost, in all his uniqueness and wonder, is tragic.[5]

There is no sin in worldly success per se. But because worldly success is such a seductive idol, God in His wisdom will make it impossible for worldly success to satisfy—either by withholding it, removing it, or giving you so much that you gag on it.

The problem is that if you or I could find satisfaction in worldly success apart from God, we would. So to protect us from our

4. Cited in Walter Kaufmann, *Existentialism from Dostoevsky to Sartre* (New York: New American Library, 1975), 345–360.

5. Francis A. Schaeffer, *Escape from Reason* (Downers Grove, Ill.: InterVarsity Press, 1968), 90.

own sinful natures, God in His grace frustrates our ambitions when they would destroy us.

Enjoy nice things if and when you can. But beware of this problem: All the known benefits of power, position, prestige, pleasure, possessions, and prosperity are *temporal*, but all the risks are *eternal*. It makes no difference if these risks are known or unknown; they are still risks. So why take a chance?

The secular worldview poses a double question: How much pleasure would it take for you to gamble that this life is all there is? How much pain could you endure if you had faith that God would take care of you?

A secular belief system breaks down because, as we all learn eventually, a life focused on becoming "happy, healthy, and wealthy" just doesn't satisfy. At some point we realize, *There must be more to life than this. There's gotta be.*

A Moral Belief System

For me, that realization came in the Army when I woke up in a ditch in my car with a hangover. I thought to myself, *What happened to you, Morley? You wanted your life to count. But you're just a nobody headed nowhere.* At that precise moment, my secular worldview collapsed.

Shortly after that, in a freshman Lit course, I read in Shakespeare's *Hamlet*, "This above all: to thine own self be true, and it must follow, as the night the day, thou canst not then be false to any man."

It was a defining moment. I thought, *That's the most noble idea I've ever heard!* So I adopted that as my new life credo and, on that day, became a moralist.

The decision to step into a moral system is the decision to be "a good boy" or "a good girl" and try to do what's right.

> *We all learn eventually, a life focused on becoming "happy, healthy, and wealthy" just doesn't satisfy.*

C. S. Lewis noted that all human beings acknowledge some kind of morality. In other words, they feel toward certain proposed actions a feeling captured by the words "I ought" or "I ought not."[6] To live by this sense of "ought-ness" is the most noble thought of the moral belief system.

Filled with fresh passion and revived motives, the moralist abandons self in an

---

6. C. S. Lewis, *The Problem of Pain* (New York: Macmillan, 1962), 21.

admirable attempt to leave the world a better place. Full of optimism, the moralist believes the world can be set right. Our impulse or instinct is to do something good for ourselves and others. If the highest value of the secular person is *pleasure,* the devotion of the moral person is *do the right thing*.

Joining a church may well be part of this system—Jesus is a wonderful example to follow, after all. It is very important to "look" good. A church membership can't hurt.

Morality is an exhausting experience because it turns out that we can never be as good as we thought we could make ourselves. What's more, our own nasty secrets keep rearing their ugly heads. As C. S. Lewis noted, all moral systems "agree in prescribing a behavior which their adherents fail to practice. All men alike stand condemned, not by alien codes of ethics, but by their own."[7]

We are at a loss to explain the gaping holes in our integrity, why we lack genuine power and, despite wanting to do right, why we continue to experience frequent and inevitable failure.

There may be successes along the way, but not enough to cover up the anomalies, as the following story illustrates.

7. Lewis, *The Problem of Pain,* 21.

The Rogers Kirven Story

As an investment banker, Rogers Kirven got tired of watching other men take his advice and get rich. So nine years after he began his career, Rogers started his own company and plunged into the world of accomplishment, accumulation, and recognition.

By the age of forty-four, Rogers had met his goal—a net worth in the top one percent of the United States. "I'm a counter," he confessed. "I keep score and in this case, it was money."

Then Rogers received an unsolicited offer to sell. "My first impulse," said Rogers, "was to take the money and run. Instead, I called up three friends who had sold their companies, told them I was getting ready to pull the trigger, and asked to join me for dinner to give me their advice.

"These were good moral men committed to doing the right thing—some of the most successful men in the world of business," said Rogers. "As the four of us sat at dinner, I only asked them two questions. First, 'What was your planned use of the time you would gain?' They all had versions of the same three answers:

- I want to spend more time with my soul and grow personally.

- I want to spend more time with my family.

- I want to do some things (basically toys and travel).

"Then I asked the second question: 'What is your actual use of time?' Remember these were good men with good intentions. Yet, all three had gone through a divorce since selling their companies. Each had bought a bigger toy. All were in a deep crisis of meaning."

They stepped into a stream so strong. They had no idea. They thought they were going to do the right things for the right reasons. It turned out they couldn't withstand temptation. As Mike Tyson said, "They all have a strategy until they get hit."

Fortunately for Rogers, when he sold his company he remained as the president and CEO. But the subject continued to fascinate him. Since that dinner meeting, Rogers has formally interviewed thirty-nine men who have sold their companies. Here is a summary of what he found:

- Thirty-three were divorced.

- Some who didn't have deep personal integrity had other breaches of character.

- Money and freedom had made life more fragile.

- Many took up golf, which lasted, on average, six months.

- Many bought exotic cars, which held their interest, on average, ten months.

- Many bought boats, which lasted, on average, eighteen months.

- None could robustly say their lives were better.

- All had a crisis of meaning.[8]

Why does the moral system fail? Quite simply, as hard as we try to be moral, it is not our basic nature.

Even for all of its wonderful contributions toward making the world a better place, the moral system, in the end, has no power to deliver us from our darkest thoughts and deeds. You can be walking to a podium to receive a plaque that acknowledges your service to the community, and at the same time be lusting over someone else's spouse sitting in the front row.

---

8. Personal correspondence.

We can make progress, but at our core we are selfish and sinful. Even the good we do just never seems good enough. This system is a black hole that swallows up everything we give it, and then demands more.

Eventually the moral system collapses under the weight of a million little lies. You just cannot keep pretending forever. It simply isn't working out. The spirit was willing, but the flesh was weak.

When we finally realize our "bad deeds" are more than a few minor anomalies, the moral system begins to break apart. Perhaps you destroyed the trust of your spouse. Maybe you have driven your children away. It begins to dawn on us that we cannot become who we want to be without "outside" assistance.

Thoughts come to mind…

> Deep in my soul is
>   a question,
>   a pain,
>   a thirst,
>   a hunger,
>   a faint whisper growing stronger.
>   Is it you, God?

Humbled, anxious, we take another step—this time into the religious and spiritual sphere.

A Religious Belief System

As the anomalies of the secular and moral systems break down, the clock keeps ticking and the inward groan for relief from futility grows louder. We still want to be moral people who do good deeds, but the groan is becoming a monster. It wants to be fed.

Once we realize this groan points to a spiritual need, we begin looking to religion for the answer. The transition to a religious system is the decision to seek salvation in the spiritual realm. It is to become a "seeker."

All people have "religious experiences" at critical points in their lives. (Whether they do anything about it is, of course, a different matter.) We're all prone to wonder, *Is this all there is?*

Like C. S. Lewis, Rudolph Otto, in his book *The Idea of the Holy,* called them *numinous* experiences. Otto said that religion doesn't exclusively consist of rational assertions. We sometimes experience the holiness of God in a moment, in ways that remain inexpressible and elude description. During these encounters with God, we become profoundly aware of our "creatureliness" and, simultaneously, sense the presence of an overpowering, absolute might. Otto goes on to describe these encounters:

The feeling of it may at times come sweeping like a gentle tide, pervading the mind with a tranquil mood of deepest worship. It may pass over into a more set and lasting attitude of the soul, continuing, as it were, thrillingly vibrant and resonant, until at last it dies away and the soul resumes its 'profane,' non-religious mood of everyday experience. It may burst in sudden eruption up from the depths of the soul with spasms and convulsions, or lead to the strangest excitements, to intoxicated frenzy, to transport, and to ecstasy.... It may become the hushed, trembling, and speechless humility of the creature in the presence of—whom or what? In the presence of that which is a *mystery* inexpressible and above all creatures.[9]

Down through the centuries, this "feeling" of the existence of a Divine Being has been described by various names: *the religious instinct, the seed of religion, the sense*

9. Rudolph Otto, *The Idea of the Holy* (London: Oxford Univ. Press, 1923), 12–13.

of divinity, the numinous, or the sense of God. Personally, I like to call it the moment of humility.

In these moments, we palpably sense the presence of a Power. It is a feeling of awe, a sense of majesty, a weightiness, a feeling of gravity, or a sense of the holy. It may come by contemplating our own mortality or the greatness of God.

> All religions except Christianity are based on performance— making God happy, or at least avoiding His wrath.

We become religious when we decide to combine this Divine Power, for which we feel awe, with our moral system. In a religious belief system, our ideas about right and wrong become governed by a God who is the guardian of the morality to which we feel obligation.[10] If the devotion of the secular person is *pleasure* and the devotion of the moral person is *do the right thing*, then the devotion of the religious person is *good deeds to please God*.

---

10. Discussed in C. S. Lewis, *The Problem of Pain* (New York: Macmillan, 1962), 22.

Performance for God

Instead of doing good deeds to earn favor with *men*, the religious person does good deeds to earn favor with *God*. The religious person thinks, *If I can just be good enough and do enough good deeds, then God will accept me, or at least not punish me.* That's because all religions except Christianity are based on perfor- mance—making God

> *Religious systems are perfectly designed to produce despair.*

happy, or at least avoiding His wrath. How well you do is up to you, based on things such as your obedience to strict codes of behavior or the quality of your sacrifices.

The focus of a religious system is *out- ward* behavior and performance rather than an *inward* change of heart. Unfortunately, religious systems are perfectly designed to produce despair, because no matter how much this person does, it is never enough. Mike, a father of four kids, said, "I put every- thing into it. I ushered during worship services and served on a committee in my church, but then got tired of that. Religion wore me out, so I said to myself, 'I'll just put that effort in at work.' Now it's ten years later, and I'm nowhere."

In the end, the religious system is really nothing more than an exhausting attempt to please God in our own strength. But that kind of religion never seems to be enough or have any real power to completely overcome sinful behavior. Technically, this is called "works righteousness."

The religious person stands on the fringe of Christianity. This person has tried to be good and has tried to obey God—but without power. They have tried to "deserve" or "earn" that which can only be had as a gift. Still perplexed by secret sins, he or she has yet to feel like a beggar standing in the presence of a holy God. Instead, they are trying to satisfy the demands of their God or gods through their own efforts.

Is This How You Feel?

Dear God:

If there is a God. Oh, I don't actually doubt the existence of God—not really. True enough, I would like to see, even feel, the weight of the evidence for His existence. But I don't really doubt there is a God. My problem is more practical. I'm lonely. I feel isolated. Empty. Disillusioned.

I don't know the state of my soul. It concerns me. I've done some things I regret, but I don't want to be separated from God forever because of them. But even more, I don't want to live like this anymore. Something needs to change. Something's got to give.

I've tried to live a good life—a moral life, but it's not working out. I don't seem to be able to control my destructive emotions. Ironically, the more I care for someone, the more I seem to hurt them. Some of the things I say to those I love the most baffle me—I can be so negative.

To be honest, I'm proud. My pride is killing me. I pretend to know things I don't. I've been religious, but it just seemed like another way of saying, "Do this," and "Don't do that." I've been judgmental of people who use Christianity as a crutch. I've ridiculed my Christian friends and associates for being weak. But, hey, I'm feeling pretty weak right now myself. Frankly, I could use a crutch.

Sometimes I feel like I'm nothing but a piece of meat. I feel like a product that people use, and then discard. Is there anyone who cares about "me"—just me, not what I can do for them? God, I think that would be You.

I've picked up this book because, if You're really there and if You will have me, I really need You in my life. I want to come home. My simple, honest prayer is this: I confess that I have been living by my own ideas. It hasn't worked out. I am ready, even eager, to come home to You. But in all honesty, I do not know who You are—not really; I've created the illusion that I do, so it's going to take some courage on my part to admit that I've been wrong— courage I'm not sure I have. I'm asking You to give me the strength I need in order to take this step.

I want to know You as You are, not as a figment of my imagination. Not like the caricatures I see on television. Not in a man-made way, but as You really are. I open

*my mind to You, and I ask that you
open Your heart to me. With this
prayer, I ask You to reveal the truth
to me. Amen.*

"True" Truth

One day after using a bar of soap I asked my
wife to buy a different brand. "What kind do
you want?" she asked.

"I don't know," I answered. "All I know is
that this is not it."

That's how most people end up feeling
about their belief systems.

Christianity claims that it will get you over
that "hump" and solve the
problem of futility. That in
itself is not unusual, since
all systems make this same
claim. But if your system
has been secular, moral,
or religious, you've probably already concluded that

> *The best counter-
> feit is the one that
> looks the most like
> the real thing.*

the anomalies just don't add up—"that this
is not it." Your worldview has traces of truth,
but it's not *the whole truth and nothing but
the truth*—what theologian Frances Schaeffer
liked to call "true" truth.

Which counterfeit bill makes it successfully into circulation? Isn't it the one that

looks most like the real thing? Just as people unwittingly accept counterfeit bills, we often adopt systems that don't deliver because they *can't* deliver; they're not the real thing.

Can the Christian system, though, really solve the problem of futility? Is it really the "true" truth?

Chapter 4

The Christian Belief System

People are naturally suspicious of things they have never properly understood. Christianity is no exception. C. S. Lewis once said of the atheists and agnostics he debated, "Our opponents had to correct what seemed to us their almost bottomless ignorance of the faith they supposed themselves to be rejecting."[11] Pascal made a similar observation: "Let them at least learn what this religion is which they are attacking before attacking it."[12]

Confusing a Little Knowledge for a Lot

Each summer I study a subject completely unrelated to my vocation. For example, I've studied sailing, sculling, interior design, bodybuilding, container gardening, and epistemology. It's a nice diversion.

---

11. C. S. Lewis, *God in the Dock* (Grand Rapids: Eerdmans, 1970), 127.

12. Blaise Pascal, *Pensées*, # 427 (London: Penguin Books, 1966), 155.

In the process I usually end up knowing more than most people about the subject under my microscope—at least for the next several months. However, I usually fall prey to a common mistake. Because I know more about my study subjects than most people, it's easy to think I know more than I really do. The tendency is to confuse knowing a little with knowing a lot.

Can you remember how embarrassing it is to act like a know-it-all around someone, and then discover you're talking to a person who *really* knows what they're talking about? I can. I remember confidently telling my sister-in-law about a football player for the Miami Dolphins—something I'd read in the paper. I was feeling pretty smug...until she quoted his college record, year-to-date performance, and family information. A real fan can make a pretender feel like a fool.

It's the same with Christianity. Our tendency, if we're not careful, is to think that because we know a little, we know more than we actually do.

Pseudo-Christianity: Inoculation

Some commentators suggest that America has become a *post*-Christian culture, a *formerly* Christian nation. However, most

Americans still consider themselves Christians—several polls show around 80 percent of Americans make the claim. One poll humorously revealed 88 percent of Americans are sure they are going to heaven, but only 67 percent are sure heaven exists. So 21 percent are sure they are going to a place they are not sure exists!

Perhaps it would be better to say that we live in a *pseudo*-Christian culture. A pseudo-Christian culture is a non-Christian culture that thinks it is Christian. A pseudo-Christian is someone who is Christian by *custom* rather than *conviction.*

I know from my ministry work that many men become part of a Christian church but don't really know what's going on. Although they are often regulars at church—and sometimes even pillars—many are too embarrassed to admit they don't really get it. They know enough of the lingo to make it seem like they know what they don't really know.

Many people *think* they have heard the true gospel, found it wanting, and have rejected it, when in fact they have yet to hear it. What they've heard instead are enough sound bites and clichés to inoculate them against the real thing. Like getting a flu shot, they've only heard enough of the gospel to make them immune to the true message of Christ.

Getting a Fair Trial

It would not be intellectually honest to never give Christianity a fair trial and then claim it doesn't work. If you became a true Christian, accepted the gift of faith, and *then* it didn't work, *then* you would have a basis for honestly rejecting it.

I can understand if someone, after making a thorough and honest investigation, correctly understands Christianity and decides to reject it. That passes every test of honesty I can think of. The person I worry about, and would like to challenge, is the one who rejects Christianity without ever understanding it. Let's at least make sure that if anyone rejects Christianity, they are rejecting what it actually is.

> *Let's at least make sure that if anyone rejects Christianity, they are rejecting what it actually is.*

To understand the Christian belief system we must first have the correct information. No jury ever gave their verdict until they first heard the evidence.

What Is True Christianity?

Describing Christianity reminds me of the old story about three blind men describing an elephant. One grabbed its leg and said, "It's like a tree." Another grabbed the trunk and said, "It's like a hose." The third grabbed an ear and said, "It's like a great fan." All true, but only partially.

Our task here is much simpler: What is the minimum description of Christianity that still explains the whole? The risk in explaining the faith that Jesus proclaimed is to add any extra test or rule of behavior that Jesus did not.

Christianity itself helps us at this point by breaking itself down into two parts: "the gospel" (the Greek word *kerygma*) and "the teachings" (the Greek word *didache*). You don't need to know how an engine works in order to drive a car. Likewise, you don't need to know all the Christian teachings in order to become a Christian. You only need to understand the gospel, often called "the Good News."

The Gospel

Everything I am about to mention can be confirmed by attending a service at any Bible-believing Christian church anywhere in the world this coming Sunday morning. Read the bulletin, the words to the hymns or choruses, and the creeds. Listen to the

Scripture reading, the prayers, and the sermon. Everything can be found there.

Here is the gospel in a nutshell: The Bible declares that two thousand years ago, in the fullness of time, God's love for mankind moved Him to send His Son, Jesus, as an atoning sacrifice for our sins. Christianity *is* Jesus Christ. Through faith in Jesus, our sins are forgiven and we receive the promise of an abundant life and eternal salvation.

These claims, of course, are either true or they are not true. At this point, however, I am not asking you to believe Christianity—only to understand it.

Everything we know about Christianity can be traced back to the Bible. The simplest expression of the gospel is quoted by the apostle Paul: "For the wages of sin is death, but the gift of God is eternal life in Christ Jesus our Lord" (Romans 6:23). In this verse we see three things. The first is *the problem of mankind,* the second is *the issue of Jesus,* and the third is *the gift of eternal life.*

These three elements of the gospel have traditionally had formal names: *the doctrine of man, the doctrine of Christ,* and *the doctrine of salvation.* Here's a way to summarize this message, and the Christian belief system, that's easy to remember:

Adam and Eve failed (the problem of mankind)

Jesus nailed (the issue of Jesus)

Grace prevailed (the gift of eternal life)

Let's briefly look at these three parts.

Adam and Eve Failed

Christianity teaches that a catastrophe took place in the Garden of Eden. Evil entered the world, and people began to make sinful choices. Adam and Eve began a downward spiral of sin that continues to the present day.

Christianity teaches that God is holy and perfect, and that all people are guilty of sin against Him, which halts our progress toward an abundant life. Not only is progress halted, but we also have become alienated from our Creator. No one is innocent.

> *No matter what you've done, you can be forgiven.*

It is this gap—between our sinful state and the abundant life—that creates futility. Futility would not be so horrific if we did not know by instinct what we had lost.

The true tragedy of our existence is not what we have become, but what we could have been. We all sense by intuition that mankind has not reached its potential. We each have an instinct that tells us the human race was destined for better, that our dignity has been tarnished. Logic tells us that something catastrophic has happened to mankind.

In the first chapter, the question was posed, "Why am I still so restless?" Saint Augustine gave the answer in the first paragraph of his book *The Confessions*: "You have made us for Thyself, and our hearts are restless until they rest in Thee."

The core message of Christianity is that no matter how futile your life has become, Jesus Christ wants to restore you to your original dignity and give you rest for your soul both now and forever. This is true Christianity: No matter what you've done, you can be forgiven.

Jesus Nailed

Christianity is based on an historical event.

Christianity offers two compelling reasons why God sent his Son to become a human being. First, He reduced Himself to human flesh so that we might comprehend Him (the *Incarnation*). Second, Jesus offered a final, perfect sacrifice for our sins (the *Atonement).*

The *history* of Jesus is the story of his *Incarnation.* Jesus was a living person who existed in history, performed remarkable miracles, claimed deity, and was resurrected from death. If the birth, life, death, and resurrection of Jesus had never happened in history, there would be no Christian religion.

The Jesus of history is also the Christ of faith. The *doctrine* of Christ—He died for our sins—is that Jesus Christ is the Savior who made *Atonement* for our sins. He satisfied the "wages of sin is death" problem (see Romans 6:23). Why do we need a Savior? We wouldn't need a Savior if we had done nothing wrong.

This good news (gospel) about Jesus and His salvation is the message of the Bible. "God promised this Good News long ago through his prophets in the holy Scriptures. The Good News is about his Son" (Romans 1:2-3 NLT).

> *God has done for love what He would do for no other reason.*

The Bible makes a beeline to Jesus. "Salvation is found in no one else, for there is no other name under heaven given to men by which we must be saved" (Acts 4:12).

Jesus Christ died for our sins and our salvation. "So Christ was sacrificed once to take away the sins of many people; and he will appear a second time, not to bear sin, but to bring salvation to those who are waiting for him" (Hebrews 9:28).

The unique purpose of the Bible is to lead us to salvation through Jesus Christ. John 20:30-32 says, "Jesus did many other miraculous signs in the presence of his disciples, which are not recorded in this book. But these are written that you may believe that Jesus is the Christ, the Son of God, and that by believing you may have life in his name."

God has done for love what He would do for no other reason. "But because of his great love for us, God, who is rich in mercy, made us alive with Christ even when we were dead in transgressions—it is by grace you have been saved" (Ephesians 2:4-5).

The Father's redeeming love through Christ, retold in countless ways, is the great story of the Bible.

The unmistakably unique claim of Christianity is that no matter what a person has done, where they have been, or how long they've been gone, a merciful and loving God longs for them to come home. "God our Savior...wants all [people] to be saved

and to come to a knowledge of the truth"
(1 Timothy 2:3-4).

In His own words, Jesus said, "I came that
you may have life and have it abundantly. I
came to seek and to save the lost. For God
so loved that world that he sent me into the
world so that whoever believes in me will not
perish but have everlasting life. I tell you the
truth, whoever hears my words and believes
him who sent me has eternal life and will not
be condemned; he has crossed over from
death to life.

"All that the Father gives me will come to
me, and whoever comes to me I will never
drive away. I shall lose none of them that he
has given me, but raise them up at the last
day. My sheep know my voice, and no one
can snatch them out of my hand." About His
identity, Jesus said, "He who has seen me has
seen the Father. The Father and I are one. I
who speak to you am the Messiah."[13]

Why a Human?

You might imagine that if God had, say, one
hundred characteristics, that in Jesus you
might see ten characteristics on display.
It's not like that at all. The Christian system

---

13. See John 10:10; Luke 19:10; John 3:16; 5:24; 6:37, 39;
10:27-28; 14:9; 10:30; 4:26.

teaches that Jesus is "the exact representa-tion" of God's being, all of God in a human body, and that seeing Jesus is the same as seeing the Father.[14] This doesn't mean we can know everything about God, but that noth-ing about the nature or character of God in any way conflicts with Jesus, and vice versa. He really is "all the fullness of God in a human body" (Colossians 2:9 NLT).

How can this be? A favorite story of unknown origin illustrates the Incarnation of Jesus.

Flurries of snow swirled on a chilly Christmas Eve. Standing at the front window, a man waved as his wife and children drove away to attend the candlelight service. He couldn't understand all the fuss about Jesus.

Alone, he busied himself decorating the family tree. Suddenly, he heard a "thump" against the window, and then another, and another, "thump...thump." He looked out, and there, shivering on the ground out-side the window, lay several tiny sparrows attracted by the light and warmth inside.

Touched, the man went to the garage, turned on the light, and opened the door. The birds didn't move. He got behind them and tried to shoo them in. They scattered.

14. See Hebrews 1:3; Colossians 2:9; John 14:9.

He made a trail into the garage by crumbling some crackers. They wouldn't budge.

He was frustrated as it sunk in that he was a giant, alien creature who terrified the tiny birds. Why couldn't he make them understand that what he wanted more than anything was to help them?

Disheartened, the man went back inside and stared out the window at the frightened little birds. Then, like a bolt of lightning, a thought struck him. *If only I could become a little bird myself—for just a moment. Then they wouldn't be afraid, and I could show them how to find warmth and safety.*

Suddenly it dawned on him. *Now I understand. That's why Jesus came.*

The Screen People

Physicist Hugh Ross cleverly illustrated the same point. Imagine a couple of two-dimensional people who live on your computer screen—a couple of "stick figures," or "screen people."

Suppose you, living in three dimensions, are sitting with your face eight inches away from the screen. To the screen people, who can only see in height and width, you are invisible. Now suppose you wanted to make yourself known to the screen people. How would you do it? First, you could touch your finger to the screen. How would you be perceived? The screen people would think you were a dot. And when you removed your finger, you would once again be invisible to them.

Now suppose you wanted to try again, so this time you placed your finger lengthwise on the screen. How would you be perceived? The screen people, perceiving only height and width, would think you were a line. Next, imagine that you could actually push your hand through the screen—that it was like a liquid surface. If you pushed your finger through, the screen people would perceive that you were a circle. If you kept pushing your arm through, they would perceive you as a bigger circle. But because they are unable to perceive in the third dimension, they will never perceive you as you are. The only way to communicate with them on their level would be to somehow reduce yourself to two dimensions and become a screen person. Then they could perceive you.

Ross makes the point that God, who has many more dimensions than we do, no doubt does interact with us in the same way we might interact with screen people—which would explain why people perceive God so differently, depending on what "part" of His other dimensions He happens to be revealing at the time.

The unique claim of Christianity, however, is that not only does God relate to us from His multidimensionality, but He has also reduced Himself in His Son Jesus to become, in effect, a screen person so that we might comprehend Him.[15]

Grace Prevailed

Becoming a Christian is not about "doing" something but about acknowledging one's inability to do *anything* to save oneself. It's not about modifying your behavior to make God happy.

One day, Mark was explaining Christianity to Chase. Chase was interested and said, "But I have nothing to offer!"

"You're beginning to understand," said Mark.

> *The principle requirement for becoming a Christian is to admit that you are not worthy to be one.*

A woman said, "I don't feel like I'm worthy of God." She is close, very close, to understanding Christianity.

---

15. Hugh Ross, *Beyond the Cosmos* (Colorado Springs: NavPress, 1996), 74–76, 89–100.

The principal requirement for becoming a Christian is to admit that you are not worthy to be one. Christians say it like this: "I confess that I am a sinner who needs a Savior."

The work of salvation is a work of *grace*. The apostle Paul wrote, "But because of his great love for us, God, who is rich in mercy, made us alive with Christ even when we were dead in transgressions—it is by *grace* you have been saved" (Ephesians 2:4-5, emphasis added).

Christianity is unique among all religions because it is the only religion based on non-performance. Once this simple idea called *grace* is grasped, it begins a chain reaction in the soul. There is no merit to be earned. Rather than receiving justice, we have through God's mercy received grace, which leads to godly sorrow and to faith.

The New Testament declares this:

> Therefore, if anyone is in Christ, he is a new creation; the old has gone, the new has come! All this is from God, who reconciled us to himself through Christ...God was reconciling the world to himself in Christ, not counting men's sins against them....God made him who had no sin to be sin for us, so that in him we might

become the righteousness of God.
(2 Corinthians 5:17-19, 21)

This is the Christian belief system. Again, at this point, I'm not asking you to believe Christianity—only understand it.

Personal Reflection

Now that we've completed the overview of these four belief systems, I would like to invite you to sit quietly for a moment and reflect.

Picture your life recorded on a single sheet of paper. Suppose the front side is the first half of your life, and the back is the second half. Some percentage of your "life script" has already been written—whether a quarter, a third, a half, or more. The rest is blank—waiting to be written. Ask yourself, "Where did I come from? Where am I going? What is the purpose of my life?"

What else can we learn from this sheet of paper? First, think for a moment about the past. Are you surprised by the path your life has taken? What are the belief systems you have embraced?

Second, think about the present. Was this the script you set out to write, and why or why not? Are you happy with the way the script has turned out so far?

Are you ready for a change? To change, you have to become uncomfortable with something about your current situation. But you also have to have confidence in the thing you are changing to.

So in the next chapter we'll explore some of the common questions and doubts that hold people back from realizing that it's very reasonable to believe Christianity.

Part Two:

Common Questions and Objections

Chapter 5

The Existence of God—Is the Idea of God Logical?

Once I saw a poster of deep outer space taped in a hallway leading to a high school cafeteria. The caption read: *Either we are alone in the universe or we are not. Both ideas are overwhelming.*

The Idea of No God: What If We Are Alone?

Are we alone? Is it true that God has given no proof of His existence? Is God just something we have created to take care of a psychological need?

Most philosophers, scientists, and theologians did not debate the question of God's existence until the last few centuries, as scientific knowledge gained stature and philosophy engendered a climate of skepticism. It seems the more we know, the more confused we become. These debates over God's existence leave a lot of good people doubtful, especially with new ideas streaking across the globe at digital speed.

There are, of course, skeptics who will never accept what's proven, much less what's probable. But what can we offer people who are open to considering a reasonable explanation but have sincere, honest doubts? What constitutes "reasonable proof?"

What Is Reasonable Proof?

In a court of law there are two different standards of proof, depending on whether the case is criminal or civil. The lowest burden of proof is for a civil case, such as a contract dispute. In a civil case, the plaintiff must only prove "a preponderance of the evidence," so a jury can render a verdict even though doubt remains.

In criminal cases, however, the prosecutor must prove his or her case "beyond and to the exclusion of every reasonable doubt." The most brutal judgment our judicial system can render is capital punishment; you cannot punish a person more severely than taking his or her life. However, even for the most severe form of punishment, the standard is not *absolute* proof, but the exclusion of reasonable doubt.

Here's the point: neither of these two standards of proof requires the 100-percent elimination of all doubt. Instead, the jury or judge must apply wisdom to the evidence they are given, and then make a reasoned decision.

In this book, we will hold to the higher standard of proof. Our goal is to eliminate reasonable doubt. I'll present a progression of probabilities and proofs that will hopefully help you move from the idea that Christianity is *possible* to the realization that it is *plausible*, then even *probable*, and finally to a *"beyond a reasonable doubt"* belief.

Some of the most brilliant skeptics in history, once they decided to make an investigation of Christianity, have found reasonable proof for the existence of God and the deity of Jesus Christ. Let's turn our attention to some of the proofs.

The Idea of God

Let's begin by asking you to picture "the world" in your mind. You may want to picture your community, the United States, the earth, our solar system, or the universe. You may choose to picture the world of your relationships. Any of these will work. Whatever comes to your mind, focus on that picture for a few seconds until you see it clearly.

Next I'd like to ask you a question, one you have no doubt already considered many times: Where did this world come from? Ponder this for a moment.

When we picture the world, we are not forced to conclude that the world is necessary. There is no necessary reason why there is "something" instead of "nothing."

> *If you saw a cake on the counter, you would never think it got there by itself.*

Nonetheless, there is "something," so when we ask, "Where did it come from?" it is natural to be struck with the idea that it had to come from "somewhere." This leads us by intuition[16] to the idea of a *Necessary Power or Being*, which most people call God.

Let me give an example. If you walked into your kitchen and saw a cake on the counter, you would immediately conclude that someone had put it there. You may be surprised that there is a cake rather than no cake, but once you have seen it, you would never think it got there by itself. You would know that it was *necessary* for someone to have been in your kitchen.

---

16. Here, I mean intuition the way Descartes used it to describe how we can arrive at an idea with such absolute clarity that it can be taken as a certain truth, which can be immediately apprehended by anyone.

I clearly remember the first time this intuition dawned on me. It happened in college. I was lying in the grass on my back, looking into the night sky. My eyes were feasting on a dazzling display of stars. Suddenly the mystery of it all became overwhelming. I felt like such an ant. I felt so small and contingent. It was at that moment that the idea of a Necessary Being hit me. Since I was raised in a Protestant church, my exact thought was, *For this to exist, it is necessary for God to exist.*

Although I grew up in a church and had been taught I should believe in God, that was the first time it occurred to me that it was impossible for a Necessary Being to *not* exist. And so, as nearly all except the most radical skeptics have done, I chose to accept the inescapable deduction that there exists a Necessary Being.

I'm not yet suggesting we've established whether this Necessary Being is a machine, a spirit, or a personal being. For Aristotle, the "being" was the Uncaused Cause (or sometimes the Unmoved Mover). Some people think of this Necessary Being as a great watchmaker who wound up the world and is no longer involved. A few people think of it as a mechanistic, impersonal "Matrix-like" force. Since most people refer to this

Necessary Being by the name God, we will use the term God from this point forward.

I'm only trying to make this one point: Because the world exists, all people through intuition can believe the idea that God must exist necessarily.

When Russia abandoned seventy years of atheistic communism, one high-ranking official said, "All these years they have told us there is no God. But we have always known that was not true. Even though they erased the memory of God from our schoolbooks, they could not erase Him from our genetic memory."

> *"Facts do not cease to exist because they are ignored."*
> —Aldous Huxley

If you accept the idea of a Necessary Being—that God must exist necessarily—that is all I'm asking you to presuppose. This, however, is a huge step, a step based on certain and indisputable deductive reasoning.

On the other hand, if you already believe *more* than the idea of a Necessary Being, that may or may not be an advantage because Christianity is just as likely to be misunderstood as understood. So there may be times when you will need to reconsider some things you thought you had already settled.

Once you are struck by this intuition, you may choose to believe it or not—but it is still true. As English essayist and atheist Aldous Huxley once said, "Facts do not cease to exist because they are ignored." God is who He is, and whether we believe it or not is immaterial to whether or not He exists, or to what He is like.

What kind of Entity or Being could create this universe?

What Can Be Known About God Through Observation and Intuition

We all make mistakes in our thinking so our rational contemplation won't always be spot-on, but what God is like can still be deduced by contemplating the work he has done in creation. Consider these examples.

The naked cosmos should be much too harsh for life—the vast freezing-cold vacuum of space, the desolate asteroids and planets, the extreme heat and unfiltered harmful rays of billions of suns. Yet the earth has air, rain, crops, food, and many joyful hearts. Most of us don't have to gasp for air, or always be thirsty, or waste away from hunger. Whether gazing into the evening sky, appreciating the intricacies of the human eye, marveling over the miracle of human birth, or observing the delicate balance of the environment, we, by intuition, conclude there must be a purpose to it all. Nature is simply too enchanting and marvelous to be random.

As a painting reveals something about its painter or a poem reveals something about its poet, so the creation reveals something about its creator. We would always assume that the *character* of any creator is in some way revealed in his creation. For example, a building reflects something of what the architect is like. This hospitable environment in a hostile cosmos suggests a God who cares for His creatures.

Here's another example. As previously said, all the people groups history has known have acknowledged some kind of morality, captured by phrases like *I ought* and *I ought not*. Suppose someone got on a plane, opened the overhead bin, and removed someone else's suitcase and placed it in the aisle to make room for his or her own. All people would feel the injustice—the "ought not"—of such an action. Through contemplation we can ask, "Where did this sense of 'ought-ness' come from?" The logical intuition is that the attributes of the creature must be attributable to its creator, who is, therefore, *moral*.

Julian of Norwich, a fourteenth-century Christian mystic in England, once pictured something in the palm of her hand the size of a hazelnut. She recounted that when she asked, "Lord, what is it?" God replied, "This is all that ever has been created."[17] The earth is a pebble in the palm of God's hand. We are struck by the intuition that God must be indescribably powerful.

> *The most simple explanation for the existence of the Creation is that there is somewhere a Creator.*

All of us have moments when we are overwhelmed with a sense of gratitude for our blessings, however magnificent or meager they might be. Feeling grateful is linked to an intuition that we have received something beyond what we deserve—a gift that must come from a giver.

We have all experienced the joy of love, parenting, doing useful work, providing for a family, or enjoying relaxing days—an accumulation of experiences that seem to say there is something intrinsically valuable about the human experience, and that the giver of such life must be good.

17. Julian of Norwich, *Revelations of Divine Love* (London: Penguin Books, 1966), 68.

When we gaze into the bejeweled evening sky, what are those twinkling stars trying to say? They utter, "There is so much more that you do not know. The cosmos is so big, and you are so small. Yet, look at how magnificently you have been made. We stars didn't just appear. Where do you think we came from?"

> *Which is more reasonable—to require proof that there is a Creator, or proof that there is not?*

Occam's Razor is the theory that the most simple explanation tends to be correct. Creation exists. Creatures exist. The most simple explanation for the existence of the Creation is that there is somewhere a Creator. If there were no cake, we would say there was no need for a baker. But since there is a cake, there must necessarily be a baker.

Where there is a Design there must be a Designer. Where there is Purpose there must be a Reason. There is somewhere an Architect, a Painter, a Sculptor, a Poet, whose imagination and ability vastly exceed the limits of our human comprehension.

Which seems more reasonable to you—to require proof that there is a Creator, or proof that there is not? Given what we can see with our own eyes, someone who claims there is no God has a much higher burden of proof. As G. K. Chesterton aptly said, "If there were no God, there would be no atheists."

All of this visible evidence of God is sometimes referred to as *general revelation*—what God has revealed about himself to all people "in general." Here's what the Bible says we can know about God through what we see for ourselves: "For since the creation of the world God's invisible qualities—his eternal power and divine nature—have been clearly seen, being understood from what has been made…" (Romans 1:20).

I hope at this point you agree, but what if you still have doubts? God offers no coercive evidence for His own existence, which He could have easily done, so that seekers must inevitably come to believe by faith.

Pascal's Wager

Let's suppose for a moment that you agree in principle that it's more rational to believe than not, but you still can't bring yourself to do so. Do you have any options? Yes, in that case you can make French philosopher Blaise Pascal's famous wager.

According to Pascal, every person must make a wager—heads or tails—whether God is, or isn't.

If you wager heads that God exists, you can either win or lose. If you lose, you lose only what you were going to lose anyway, so you are not putting anything additional at risk. In essence, you have risked nothing. But if you win, you win everything—eternal life and infinite happiness.

On the other hand, if you bet tails that God does not exist, you can also either win or lose. If you win—God doesn't exist—you win only what you already have, so there really is nothing to gain. However, if you lose, and God does exist, then your loss is immeasurable.

So, on rational grounds alone, you have no choice except to bet heads (that God does exist), because you stand to win an infinite gain if you have wagered correctly, and have nothing to lose you wouldn't lose anyway. To do otherwise is to renounce reason.

> *It takes just as much faith to not believe in God as to believe—perhaps more.*

The point of this wager is not so much to inspire you to suddenly abandon all doubt and embrace faith. Rather, the point is simply to demonstrate that belief in God is the most reasonable response.

And yet, many who claim to not believe in God because of reason simply ignore the facts of this wager—and the other evidence presented in this chapter—and continue to disbelieve. Why? Because their disbelief is *not* based solely on reason but is *also* a matter of faith in a different belief system. Let's be honest. With even the small amount of evidence presented in this chapter, it takes just as much faith to not believe in God as to believe—perhaps more.

But even though, as Pascal has proven, reason alone compels us to bet that God exists, reasonable people still find themselves unable to bring themselves to believe. You may be one of them. So let's soldier on and see what additional confidence we can gain by looking at the relationship between science and faith.

Chapter 6

Science—Shouldn't Science Rule Over Theology?

When the vast size of the cosmos is considered, humans are either very insignificant or very special.

Our solar system is located 26,000 light years from the center of the pinwheel-shaped galaxy we call the *Milky Way*. One light year is six trillion miles. Our sun is one of more than 200 billion stars in our galaxy, one galaxy among 100 billion or more other galaxies. It takes 226 million years for our sun to circle our home galaxy, traveling at the speed of 135 miles per second.[18] Our bodies are hurtling through space at 135 miles every second!

Our small planet is teeming with life—humans, plants, animals, reptiles, fish, birds, and insects. The conditions for life as we

---

18. These numeric values were determined in 1999 by astronomers making measurements using the *Very Long Baseline Array*, a system of ten large radio-telescope antennae placed 5,000 miles across the United States from the U.S. Virgin Islands to Hawaii. Working together as a single unit, the antennae can measure motions in the distant universe with unprecedented accuracy.

know it to exist fall within an amazingly
narrow range of values. Leading scientists
now believe that the universe is so delicately
balanced that it could not have happened by
chance.

For example, scientists have pointed out
that if the electric charge of the electron had
been even slightly different, stars wouldn't
burn. If gravity were less powerful, matter
couldn't have congealed into stars and galaxies. These forces seem minutely adjusted
to make life possible. One astronomer calls it
"a put-up job"—a great conspiracy to make
intelligent life possible.[19]

Consider the remarkable efficiency of
food chains, insect kingdoms, photosynthe-
sis, animal life, the bird and fish worlds. Not
only are these elements of creation remarkably interesting, but they also have beauty
and purpose.

To appreciate how delicately conditions
for life are balanced we need only to consider
the devastation caused by a flood, famine,
or fire. When one considers the preci-
sion required of atoms, neutrons, electrons,
quarks, and the force of gravity, and how vol-
atile conditions *could* be, the question isn't,

19. Cited in Kitty Ferguson, *Stephen Hawking: Quest for a
Theory of Everything, The Story of His Life and Work* (New
York: Bantam Books, 1991), 94.

"Why are there so many natural disasters?" but, "Why are there so few?"

Not Only Big, But Small

If, for the last 15 billion years, you had removed one molecule per second from a glass of water, you would not be able to notice any change in the water level. And a molecule may be like an entire universe of its own.

You are for all practical purposes "infinitely" larger than a molecule. You are as much larger than a molecule as the known universe is larger than you. *Cosmology,* the study of the very large, may, in the end, be eclipsed in importance by *quantum mechanics* and *string theory,* the study of the very small.

> *What goes wrong is infinitesimally small compared to what goes right.*

There are as many mysteries to be solved inside the atom as there are in the rest of the universe.

The Orderliness of Creation

Consider the regularity of sunrise and sunset, moon phases, seasons, tides, crops, forests, ecosystems, air, water, digestion, and pro-creation. I am profoundly encouraged by every sunrise—its predictability is a powerful symbol, especially when things aren't going so well. Imagine the chaos if we couldn't predict the boundaries of day and night, river and land, or winter and spring. We couldn't leave the house for a walk without a flashlight, build a house near water, or know when to plant a crop.

A person who watches a lot of news will likely wonder, *Why is there so much chaos in the world?* The nightly news draws our attention to the anomalies, but what goes wrong is infinitesimally small compared to what goes right. What is extraordinary is not that we have so *much* chaos but so *little*. If you ponder the whole of creation you can't help but wonder, *Why is there so much order in the world?*

Christianity teaches that God provides order for Creation. Acts 14:17 declares, "Yet he has not left himself without testimony: He has shown kindness by giving you rain from heaven and crops in their seasons; he provides you with plenty of food and fills your hearts with joy."

The Nature of Science

People want to know, "What is the universe all about? What is reality? What is the stuff the universe is made of?" The task of science is to explain how nature works. To do this, scientists observe nature and then form what at the time seem to be reasonable paradigms (systems) to explain what they see.

As mentioned in an earlier chapter, when too many anomalies show up, a new system emerges to replace the one that doesn't want to work anymore. There have been four major scientific para-digms in the last two thousand years— Ptolemaic, Copernican, Newtonian, and Einsteinian. In about A.D. 150 Ptolemy said,

> *Science is not really "the" truth, but an increasingly better understanding of what is true.*

"The earth is round and stationary, the center of the universe"—a geocentric universe.

Ptolemy's system prevailed for four-teen hundred years. But in 1543 Nicolas Copernicus said, "The earth is moving, and the sun is the center of the universe"—a heliocentric universe—and the Ptolemaic system collapsed. Now, of course, we know that the entire universe is in motion.

Isaac Newton built his science on the foundation of Copernicus. The "absolute" Newtonian paradigm of gravitation, motion, time, and space lasted for two hundred years. Then in the early 1900s, Albert Einstein observed "relativity" in time, space, mass, motion, and gravitation. He noticed, for example, that starlight bent as it passed near the sun, which led him to postulate a universe of curved space. Suddenly a virtually infinite number of dimensions became possible. His discoveries led to a breakup of the Newtonian paradigm.

The point is that none of these paradigms ever was (or is) "truly true." In fact, all those scientists who believed in an earth-centered or sun-centered universe were in reality wrong.

No doubt in the future, people will look at the science we today believe to be absolutely true and think of us like we think about those who believed the earth was flat. Today's science is not really "the" truth, but an increasingly better understanding of what is true.

How Science and Theology Are Related

You may be surprised to learn that science and Christianity were on friendly terms until the twentieth century. Even in the nineteenth century, when hostilities were just beginning to brew, the vast majority of scientists were adherents of Christianity—many still are.

Many twentieth-century scientists (Albert Einstein, for instance) said that Christianity and Greek-thought provide the soil that enables science to grow. Their argument has much to recommend it. First, the Christian system asserts order and design in nature. Second, Christianity creates a sense of wonder, awe, contingency, and dependency on something bigger than ourselves. Third, the Christian system asserts an open rather than a

> *Science: "How does this work?"*
> *Theology: "Why is this important?"*

closed universe, and it is responsive to explanations from beyond nature (i.e., miracles). Fourth, Christianity, unlike many Eastern religions, believes that nature is real. There is a reality out there, and we can deal with it.

In the 1950s, Einstein said, "We scientists need to get together with some theologians and see if we can shed any light together that we couldn't shed on our own." At his invitation, twelve scientists and twelve theologians met for several years. They issued a statement that scientists deal with questions of "How?" and theologians deal more with questions of "Why?" Both sides affirmed that we need the answers to both questions.[20]

---

20. For this section, I have depended on my lecture notes from Dr. Charles MacKenzie, professor of philosophy at Reformed Theological Seminary/Orlando.

Science looks at nature and asks, "How does this work?" Theology looks and asks, "Why is this important?" Science is, or should be, the friend of Christianity, and Christianity the friend of science. Christianity has nothing to fear from science; science has nothing to fear from Christianity. Science is exciting because it helps us discover more about God and His ordering of the universe.

Supernatural and Natural

The dominant scientific view today is *naturalism*—the view that the universe is a closed system. Imagine a conversation that went like this:

One day, Ted, a scientist, said to his friend Ryan, a pastor, "The problem I have with Christianity is that it depends on the Virgin Birth and the Resurrection. Now, as a scientist, I believe that natural phenomena can only be explained by natural causes."

"But just a minute, Ted," Ryan interrupted, "I also believe that natural phenomena can only be explained by natural causes."

"Well, then what about the Virgin Birth and the Resurrection?" asked Ted.

"Oh," said Ryan, "I was only trying to agree with you about natural phenomena. I also believe there are *supernatural* phenomena that can only be explained by supernatural causes. But if I get your drift, are you wanting to say that *everything* must be explained by natural causes?"

"Exactly. As a scientist, I observe nature, and I believe everything that happens must be explained by natural laws," said Ted.

"Let me ask you a question," said Ryan. "Do you believe it's possible for something to exist beyond or outside of nature? Now, before you answer, please understand my question. I'm not asking if something *does* exist, merely if it is *possible* for it to exist. Does anything *necessarily* exclude it?"

"Well, since you put it *exactly* that way," Ted said hesitantly, "I guess to be intellectually honest I would have to say that nothing can disprove the possibility. But it doesn't seem very likely."

"All right, then, but it's possible," continued Ryan. "Suppose for a moment that something beyond nature did exist—let's call it *supernatural* for debating purposes. I'm not yet saying it *does* exist, but *if* it did, could it be possible that some of the hard-to-explain phenomena we observe are actually not caused by normal laws within nature, but supernaturally? Again, don't misunderstand me. I'm not asking if you believe it, only if you can exclude it."

"Ryan, you're trying to box me in," said Ted.

"No, Ted, I'm only asking you, 'Is it possible? Does anything necessarily exclude it?'"

"Well, I feel like you're trying to trap me," said Ted. "Anyway, the answer is *no*, I cannot logically exclude the possibility."

"Well, Ted, we've made a lot of progress. You started out two minutes ago by saying that nature is a closed system. Now you have at least agreed that we know of no necessary reason why it *must* be a closed system. At least it is possible that something exists *beyond*, and, whatever it is, it could possibly act *within* the world alongside natural causes. So, I agree with you. Natural phenomena can be explained by natural causes, but, as you've now agreed, perhaps not all phenomena are caused by natural laws and interactions. If supernatural phenomena do occur, like the Virgin Birth and the Resurrection, then they could be explained by supernatural causes."

A little black cloud lingered over Ted. He looked as though he had just been bushwhacked.

"Ted, do you know why you feel like I've boxed you in? It's because you've been caught practicing theology without a license. You would dismiss me as a quack if I started drawing scientific conclusions. I would be practicing science without a license. It cuts both ways. I'll make a deal with you. I won't try to explain the natural world of science with theology if you won't try to explain the supernatural world of theology with science."

Ted muttered an answer Ryan couldn't understand.

Miracles

Miracles like turning water into wine, raising the dead, and multiplying fish and bread are impossible naturally. They cannot happen by natural causes. Christianity does not claim that they do. Everyone should understand this point.

Miracles are no more outrageous or amazing than the life of a single corn plant.

What Christianity does claim is that "other than natural" causes also exist.

Because things do happen that cannot be explained by natural causes, an "other than natural" explanation is required. The Christian system calls this "other than natural" force a *miracle.*

Hard-to-believe miracles can be made much easier to accept if we would think for a moment of all the "regular" miracles that take place all around us, which we take for granted. For example, a seed of corn smaller than a fingernail is buried in early spring, then watered and fertilized. Life appears, the corn grows knee-high by the Fourth of July, and three weeks later, there stands a six-foot-tall plant.

Though a common occurrence, doesn't the fact that the full plant resided in a small kernel have its own reality of miraculous proportions? What is the Intelligence that informs the corn plant to escape from the seed? If this act only happened once, or occasionally, would we not call it a miracle? Such as it is, it is a "regular" miracle. All things considered, the biblical miracles are no more outrageous or amazing than the life of a single corn plant.

Or consider this. When you hear about a man, Daniel, several thousand years ago interpreting dreams and surviving the night in a den of hungry lions, you might be inclined to say, "Impossible. I don't believe you. I won't believe it unless I see it with my own eyes." Or you could picture Lazarus raised from the dead, a lame man walking, or any number of other supernatural interventions into the natural order of creation.

Now, imagine for a moment that you lived back then and actually saw those miracles.

And suppose someone came to your town and prophesied to you that one day people will take coal and oil from the earth, convert it into fuel and electricity to power refrigerators, lights, air-conditioners, microwaves, automobiles, trains, and airplanes. Communication will be through books, newspapers, telephones, movies, radio, television, computers, email, the Internet, iTunes, e-books, Facebook, and smartphones.

Imagine living two thousand years ago and being regaled with stories about heart stents, chemotherapy, pacemakers, arthroscopic surgery, the concept of the United States, a Fortune 500 company, an Apple Computer store, Starbucks, and the New York Stock Exchange. What would you say? You might be inclined to say, "Impossible. I don't believe you. I won't believe it unless I see it with my own eyes."

What God did sparingly then, He does routinely today. Jesus raised a man from the dead. Now defibrillators routinely raise men from the dead every day. Jesus made a lame man walk. Today thousands of people routinely receive artificial limbs that let them walk.

What will happen in the world 2,000 years from now that today we think would take a miracle? Time travel, dematerializing matter for instant transport, worm hole travel to yet undiscovered galaxies in personal pleasure vehicles?

Disbelief in miracles depends on assuming God would limit Himself to working in only one way across all time and cultures. But why would He do that? There is nothing in the Bible or the character of God to even remotely suggest He has limited Himself to dealing uniformly with different eras.

Given the miracles we live with every day, it takes more intellectual effort to disbelieve than believe in miracles.

The Reliability of Science

As we already mentioned, since the time of Jesus, four major scientific paradigms have found prominence. Science actually has a much less stable track record than theology. Scientists understand that they may have the rug pulled out from under their theories at any time. Does it makes sense to use the less reliable to explain the more reliable? Science is a "partial" explanation of the "whole" of nature. Does it make sense to have the partial explain the whole?

> *Science actually has a much less stable track record than theology.*

Science and theology are both trying to help regular people make sense of their lives. When my father died, science could tell me *how*, but only theology could tell me *why*. Science for the body, theology for the soul.

Science *discovers* truth in nature, but science doesn't *create* truth—and has never claimed to. Christianity, on the other hand, claims that God is the Creator of all that is, and therefore all that is true.

Christianity teaches that God created and sustains the universe. Science is limited to discovering what God has already made possible. While scientists keep building bigger telescopes and more powerful microscopes (that will lead to still more paradigm changes), the Creator of the scientists offers supernatural stability. Science needs the cosmic glue of Christianity. Science changes, but Christianity remains the same.

Notice also that the "useful life" of scientific paradigms has become shorter—the Ptolemaic system lasted 1,400 years, the Copernican system 150 years, the Newtonian system 200 years, and the Einsteinian system has been around for about 100 years. Some prominent theoretical physicists believe that in the first half of the twenty-first century the two great theories of the twentieth century—*general relativity* and *quantum mechanics*—will be fused into a new paradigm, perhaps using *string theory*. As scientific knowledge increases faster and faster, will paradigms fall faster and faster? Christianity has a track record for durability. Would it not make sense to explain the "changing" by the "changeless," instead of the other way around?

When we use science to explain theology, we are using the finite to explain the infinite. The truth of archaeology, for example, is limited by what has not yet been found. It is worth mentioning that virtually every major archaeological discovery has increased the confidence of scholars in the authenticity of the Bible.

Much more so than Christianity, science has a lot of unanswered questions. For example,

- Does light travel in waves or bundles?
- If the universe is moving from order to disorder (entropy), then how can, at the same time, evolution move from disorder to order?
- If the universe is expanding in every direction and everything is moving farther away from

everything else, then where is the point from which everything is moving away—the point where Creation (a.k.a. the Big Bang) began?

Christianity is a chest full of tools, one of which is science. To be fair, science has never claimed to answer the ultimate questions. Perhaps we should fit the "partial" views of reality given by science into the more "comprehensive" view given by Christianity. As psychologist Abraham Maslow said, "If the only tool you have is a hammer, you tend to view every problem as a nail."

When faced with the vastness of the universe, some may argue, "What a waste of space!" But another can argue with equal plausibility, "Humans must be very special. All of this so that I might have life." In the end, science can still offer no bread for the deepest hungers of the soul.

Chapter 7

Evil, Futility, and Suffering— If God Is Good Why Is There So Much Suffering?

A father took his eighteen-year-old son on his very first hunting trip. He accidentally killed his son with a shotgun blast after mistaking him for a deer. In utter despair, the father then took his own life with the same gun. How can such tragedies be explained?

For many people, apparently meaningless evil is their single greatest challenge to Christian faith—like the massacre of innocent children at the Sandy Hook Elementary School in 2012. For others, it's despair over the evil they've seen personally, and the difficulties they've experienced in their own lives.

How could a good and loving God allow such things? And don't our own sufferings make us wonder…

> Does He know?
> Does He care?
> Can He do anything about it?

Except as explained in the Bible, there really are no satisfying answers for why evil, suffering, and futility exist. Within the Bible, however, there are extremely satisfying answers.

First, however, let's see how far the discussion can go without bringing in the Bible, and then we will look at what the Bible has to say.

The problem of apparently meaningless evil and suffering has both a *rational* and a *psychological* side.

The Rational Problem of Evil and Suffering

The *rational* problem of evil states that belief in God is logically inconsistent if we say that God is all-knowing, that He is all-good, that He is all-powerful—*and* that the world contains evil.[21]

Fortunately for rational thinkers, this problem has been successfully resolved by Christian philosopher Alvin Plantinga, who began by asking simply, "Where is the contradiction?" Plantinga then provided a logically possible premise that forever resolves the rational problem of evil, namely,

---

21. Known as the theistic set. Ronald H. Nash, *Faith and Reason, Searching for a Rational Faith* (Grand Rapids: Academie Books, Zondervan Publishing House. 1988), 181.

that "God created a world containing evil *and He had a good reason for doing so.*"[22] When this last phrase is added, there is no longer any contradiction with a good and all-powerful God creating a world that contains evil. While we can debate whether this is emotionally satisfying, philosophers have almost universally agreed that this is logically an irrefutable solution.

The Psychological Problem of Evil and Suffering

The other, and more difficult, concern is the *psychological* problem of evil—the apparently meaningless evil we personally observe and experience, and its effect on us. For example, a drunk driver ran a red light and senselessly killed my friend's son, Matthew. My friend has never been the same.

My own brother, Robert, died of a heroin overdose. He fought in the Army and fell into despair over the violence he saw men do to each other in war. You no doubt have your own examples.

---

22. Alvin Plantinga, *God, Freedom, and Evil* (Grand Rapids: Eeerdman's, 1974), 26. Further, he also provided his well-known free-will defense as a possible reason why God would have created such a world. Ibid, 30.

Who among us hasn't wondered how a good God could possibly allow such evil and suffering? Even though rationally there may be a perfectly reasonable explanation, *emotionally* evil raises doubts. Some people conclude that because there is evil, God probably doesn't exist.[23]

As atheist William Rowe wrote, "the variety and profusion of evil in our world, although perhaps not logically inconsistent with the existence of the theistic God, provides, nevertheless, rational support for atheism." In other words, there is so much evil in the world that, although it doesn't disprove God's existence, it undermines the basis for belief in God. [24]

Fortunately, Christianity and the Bible have a lot to say about evil and suffering that can help us come to terms with what we see in the world around us.

23. Nash, *Faith and Reason, Searching for a Rational Faith*, 195.

24. William Rowe, "The Problem of Evil and Some Varieties of Atheism," *American Philosophical Quarterly*, Volume 16 (October 1979): 335.

What Does Christianity Teach?

The Bible acknowledges and explains the
existence of evil, futility, and the suffering
that results.

First, the Bible makes it clear that in this
world everyone will suffer. Admitting evil
exists does no harm to Christian belief
because the Bible openly declares that evil
and suffering are a
normal part of life.
Even though God is not
the author of evil,
somehow He has
allowed it as part of His
larger plan.

> *The Bible describes a
> great cosmic struggle
> between the forces
> of good, evil, and
> futility.*

From Genesis to
Revelation, from cre-
ation to the present, the Bible describes a
great cosmic struggle between the forces
of good, evil, and futility that culminates
in human suffering. The prophets suffered,
Jesus suffered, the disciples suffered, and we
suffer. As a result, the atheist cannot appeal
to the presence of suffering and evil as a
contradiction to the Christian belief system.

> Dear friends, do not be surprised
> at the painful trial you are suffering,
> as though something strange were
> happening to you. (1 Peter 4:12)

> We must go through many hardships to enter the kingdom of God. (Acts 14:22)

Second, there are no instances of meaningless evil and suffering in the Bible. There is always a purpose, though it may not always be evident to those who suffer.

The *doctrine of meticulous providence* states that no evils are allowed by God unless they produce a greater good or prevent a greater evil. People can handle almost any amount of evil and suffering if they believe it is for a purpose. In every age there are countless stories of people who have suffered great financial, family, and/or health losses, only to express gratitude for God's intervention.

Here are just a few examples of purposes for suffering in the Bible:

> So that we may be delivered from bondage to decay and become children of God (see Romans 8:20-21)

> So that the work of God can be displayed in our lives (John 9:3)

> So that when we suffer, sin will lose power (1 Peter 4:1-2)

So that we will rely on God, not
ourselves (2 Corinthians 1:9)

So that our character may be
developed (Romans 5:3-5)

So that evil may be punished
(Deuteronomy 9:4-5)

So that we may be made more
sensitive to others so that we
can comfort them with the comfort we ourselves have received
(2 Corinthians 1:4 and Luke
22:31-33)

So that God may receive praise
(1 Peter 1:6-7)

Sometimes we suffer for doing right.
Sometimes we suffer for doing wrong. But
other times we suffer for no apparent reason.
For most of us, this last kind is the most difficult. For those times, isn't it encouraging to
know the Bible offers possible explanations?

That Christians suffer for no *apparent*
reason does not mean that there's no reason.
Romans 8:28 says, "And we know that in all
things God works for the good of those who
love him, who have been called according to
his purpose."

Whatever befalls the believer, it works for their good (whether in this life or eternally, only God knows). Because our sufferings have purpose and are not meaningless, there is great comfort and even joy for the believer. For example:

> Jesus said, "Here on earth you will have many trials and sorrows. But take heart, because I have over-come the world." (John 16:33 NLT)

> Therefore we do not lose heart. Though outwardly we are wast-ing away, yet inwardly we are being renewed day by day. For our light and momentary troubles are achieving for us an eternal glory that far outweighs them all. (2 Corinthians 4:16-17)

> We rejoice in the hope of the glory of God. Not only so, but we also rejoice in our suffer-ings...(Romans 5:2-3)

This, of course doesn't explain the evil that happens to the wicked. However, it should not offend anyone's rational or emotional sensibilities that the wicked experience neg-ative consequences. The Bible teaches that the Christian God is just, and the evil experienced by the wicked is fair.

Suffering still takes a significant *existential* toll on us, even if we know in our heads that evil exists. Unique among all religions, Christianity offers help for this existential problem as well. You see, the Christian God is not sitting in an ivory tower hurling lightning bolts from afar.

God isn't a disinterested spectator. He has also experienced great suffering—the greatest suffering that has ever been known. How? Christianity explains that God became a man, Jesus, to die as a sacrifice for our sins. Even though He did no wrong, He was brutally murdered. God experienced death—the death of His Son.

So, yes, God does know what you're going through. The Father has suffered. Jesus has suffered. In a mysterious way, God Himself suffered the ultimate consequences of evil so that we don't have to.

God redeemed the suffering of Jesus and made it purposeful. He has the power to redeem our suffering and make it purposeful as well. In fact, that's the great promise of Christianity.

Conclusions About Evil

Let's think about and feel the weight of the evidence.

Rationally, the existence of evil cannot prove belief in God is logically inconsistent. This is a profound argument against the claim that evil is meaningless.

Psychologically, skeptics and nonbelievers cannot prove that greater goods do not exist. Neither can theists, but believers can point to numerous possible reasons.

Biblically, the Bible declares there are no acts of meaningless evil. In fact, the Bible declares God always has a reason for allow-ing suffering. Even if we stop here and admit we don't know the rea-sons why, what follows

> *Jesus suffered and knows what we are going through.*

is of "very little interest," says Alvin Plantinga. "Why suppose if God does have good reason for permitting evil, theists would be the first to know? Perhaps God has a good reason, but that reason is too complicated to under-stand. Or perhaps he has not revealed it for some reason...."[25]

---

25. Nash, quoting Plantinga in *God, Freedom, and Evil.*

Or, as the Bible itself says, "The secret things belong to the LORD our God..." (Deuteronomy 29:29).

As mysterious as it is, Christianity offers our only real hope for the *existential* problem of evil. In Jesus, we have a God who has suffered and knows what we are going through.

So, the existence of evil actually ends up being a reason to believe in Christianity over other worldviews. Now let's return to the issue of futility, the feeling of meaningless that we all have at various points in our lives. How do we deal with that?

Back to Futility

As mentioned in Chapter 1, the third force at work in the world besides good and evil is futility. Futilities are not evils per se, but they still cause a lot of suffering.

When futility sets in, you wonder, *What's the point?* You feel that "life is a useless passion." You can sink into a deep funk of meaninglessness and frustration.

Remarkably, Christianity claims to not only *solve* the problem of futility but also to *cause* it. The Bible teaches that the whole world has been subjected to futility, frustration, vanity, and meaninglessness by God. Why? Here's how the Bible puts it:

> For the creation was subjected to
> frustration, not by its own choice,
> but by the will of the one who sub-
> jected it [God], in hope that the
> creation itself will be liberated from
> its bondage to decay and brought
> into the glorious freedom of the
> children of God. (Romans 8:20-21)

It is the Christian view that if people could find even a trace of true meaning in any earthly pursuit apart from God, they would take it. In an earlier chapter, we saw how Solomon pursued every conceivable earthly avenue to find meaning and happiness independent of God, and he came up empty.

> *Even if we get exactly what we want, we will still not be happy apart from God.*

Christianity teaches that God makes us feel the weight of futility in every worldly pursuit apart from Him—getting the big promotion, making the big bucks, living in the big house, or getting none of those things.

As we continue to seek meaning and purpose apart from God, we will eventually experience such futility that we have nowhere else to turn. God sovereignly removes any possibility of finding meaning except in Him. Futility is the chief tool by which God sovereignly draws us to Himself of our own free will.

Solomon said it this way: "I know that everything God does will endure forever; nothing can be added to it and nothing taken from it. God does it so that men will revere him" (Ecclesiastes 3:14).

> *God protects us from greater disasters than the ones we bring on ourselves.*

So even if we get exactly what we want, we will still not be happy apart from God. Apart from God, life has no meaning. That's the deal.

Futility Is Protection

Ken worked for a Fortune 100 company for eleven years. A star, he wanted the brass ring, and he was putting in the seventy hours a week required to get it. What's more, he was a deacon in his church. Ken met once a week with another man in an accountability group.

In his hunger for secular success, Ken became so busy that his accountability partner was driving Ken's son to Little League games. One day he told Ken, "You need to do something about your life. Your son is starting to be closer to me than to you." It woke him up.

We are interested in *goal* success; God is interested in *soul* success. Would we really want to get what we want if we knew it would be our undoing? Of course not. Christianity declares that an all-knowing, all-wise, all-good God actually protects us from greater disasters than the ones we bring on ourselves.

> *Not until years later did I realize that if I had gotten what I wanted, I would have self-destructed.*

Like Ken, I personally spent my twenties and thirties working and praying to achieve a business and financial success that I now realize would have destroyed me, but at the time I was disappointed I had been spared! Not until years later did I realize that if I had gotten what I wanted, I would have self-destructed. I now see that what seemed so unfair at the time was really a blessing.

The Bible contains several passages that further explain why "bad" may not be so bad after all:

> But by means of their suffering, he rescues those who suffer. For he gets their attention through adversity.... Be on guard! Turn back from evil, for God sent this

suffering to keep you from a life of
evil. (Job 36:15, 21 NLT).

When times are good, be happy;
but when times are bad, consider:
God has made the one as well as
the other.... (Ecclesiastes 7:14)

It was good for me to be afflicted
so that I might learn your
decrees....I know, O LORD, that
your laws are righteous, and in
faithfulness you have afflicted me.
(Psalm 119: 71, 75).

The Christian God is the God of love.
Christianity explains that while we work
and pray for things that would destroy us, a
loving God—like a loving parent—graciously
slows us down. We may wish He would just
leave us alone, but as C. S. Lewis noted, that
would not be asking for *more* love, but less.

We Are Easily Deceived

We are made in such a way that we want to
lead a comfortable, happy, meaningful life.
Pascal wrote these timeless words: "Despite
these afflictions man wants to be happy, only

wants to be happy, and cannot help wanting to be happy."[26]

We also are made in such a way that we think we know the best way to pull it off. But sin deceives us and, until we yield our lives to Him, we squeeze God out of our systems. The father of the Protestant Reformation, Martin Luther, once said:

> It is rightly called the deceitfulness of sin because it deceives under the appearance of good. This phrase "deceitfulness of sin" ought to be understood in a much wider sense, so that the term includes even one's own righteousness and wisdom. For more than anything else one's own righteousness and wisdom deceive one and work against faith in Christ, since we love the flesh and the sensations of the flesh and also riches and possessions, but we love nothing more ardently than our own feelings, judgment, purpose, and will, especially when they seem to be good.[27]

---

26. Blaise Pascal, *Pensées*, #134 (London: Penguin Books, 1966), 66.

27. As quoted in Philip Hughes, *A Commentary of the Epistle to the Hebrews* (Grand Rapids: Wm. B. Eerdmans Publishing Company, 1977), 149.

In order to change, we have to become uncomfortable with something. We have to come to our senses and realize that what we are striving for in life is so inferior to the abundant life God would like us to have.

> *Futility is not good, but God uses it for good.*

Christianity states that God loves us so much that He will never let us become comfortable in the world. He does this by removing the possibility of finding any meaning apart from Him.

So what's the bottom line? If God did not introduce futility into our lives and make us uncomfortable, nothing would ever change. Christianity never claims that futility is good, but that God uses it for good. Futility is the emotion that sets in when our belief system fails. It leads us to despair. Despair leads us to turn our hearts toward God. Futility is the grace of God that allows us to be disturbed out of complacency and error.

Abundance, Not Comfort

In the Christian belief system, God desires people to lead abundant lives. Yet, sadly, people often mistake abundant for *comfortable*.

Someone told the story about a farmer and his son who cleared a field together over a couple of weeks. They placed the brush in a pile, and after a few days birds came and started to build nests. When the farmer chased the birds away, his son thought he was being extremely cruel.

At the end of the two weeks, the field was cleared, and the farmer proceeded to set the pile of brush on fire. Only then did his son see that what he had thought was an act of cruelty was actually an act of kindness.

This world is not our home. Someday the world will come to an end. God doesn't want us to get too comfortable here.

A Gracious Brutality

By this point you may be thinking, *Isn't this a rather brutal system to get people to become Christians?* I suppose in one sense it is. But it's the same kind of brutality a surgeon shows who amputates a gangrenous leg in order to save the rest of the body. Christianity is a gracious belief system designed to save us.

He loves you so much that He will let you suffer, if He must, through futility or even evil, so that you will choose Him of your own free will. It is precisely because of this fierce love of God that secular, moral, and religious systems don't work. Life becomes futile when we try to tame God.

Chapter 8

The Bible—How Can You Stake Your Entire Life on Believing the Bible Is True?

The core issue about the Bible, even before the question of Christian belief is, "Am I looking at reliable data?" Since we have seen that the Bible perfectly explains both the cause and the solution to the questions raised by evil, futility and suffering, it's pretty important to know if it is also true.

A Rosetta Stone for the Soul

For more than a thousand years, ancient Egyptian written culture had been lost because we couldn't understand hieroglyphics. Then in 1799, the Rosetta Stone was discovered near the mouth of a tributary of the Nile.

The Rosetta Stone records three languages—hieroglyphics, demotic, and Greek. Scholars were able to use the Greek language to decipher the hieroglyphs and reconstruct the lost language.

Nearly all people reach a point when they feel that life is written in some undecipherable code. Søren Kierkegaard said, "The wisdom of the years is confusing. Only the wisdom of eternity is edifying."[28] He believed this "wisdom of eternity" is found in the Bible. The Bible makes the astonishing claim to decipher the mysteries of life—a Rosetta Stone for the soul.

Haven't Theologians Concluded That the Bible Isn't Reliable?

The popular press and broadcast media frequently run articles and specials about Jesus and the Bible. A particularly revealing example was ABC's special, "In Search of Jesus," hosted by Peter Jennings in June 2000. Since that time there have been a number of other shows, articles, and interviews just like it.

Most of these productions consist of "sound bite" reporting that creates doubts about the truth and reliability of the Bible. Often this type of reporting with an agenda makes it sound like only an intellectual dolt *could* believe, much less *would* believe.

I would like to answer just a handful of the questions raised by these programs and

---

28. Søren Kierkegaard, *Purity of Heart is to Will One Thing* (New York: Harper Torchbooks, 1948), 36.

articles—the same questions that tend to be raised by most secular reporting on the Bible and Christianity. You don't need to have seen any particular program to get the gist.

Are the negative things they say about Jesus and the Bible true? There are both liberal and conservative Bible scholars. Unfortunately, many of these productions only interview liberal scholars. While they acknowledge that Jesus lived, many—maybe most—liberal scholars do not believe that Jesus is who He claimed to be. Their opinions, therefore, are skewed by their worldview. (I am using *liberal* and *conservative* in a theological and not a political sense. There are, of course, many people who are both politically liberal and theologically conservative, and vice versa.)

Isn't it reasonable to assume that all Bible scholars are Christians? It isn't a requirement. Bible scholars are no more all Christians than salesmen are all extroverts.

Why do the people who are interviewed tend to be so skeptical? Everyone speaks out of their own belief system. It should not be surprising that someone whose private motivations are personal ambition, prestige, and notoriety would attribute those same motives to Jesus. They see Him attempting a political revolution. It was exactly *not* that—at least according to Jesus' own words in John 18:36: "My kingdom is not of this world. If it were, my servants would fight to prevent my arrest by the Jews. But now my kingdom is from another place."

But these people seem so persuasive, while the believers they cite are often, by and large, not believable. This is a common technique in these productions. If you had seen the ABC program mentioned above, you may have noticed that all of the comments from the skeptics were carefully selected portions of scheduled interviews with educated scholars in their areas of expertise. The unconvincing comments from the enthusiastic believers—a taxi driver, for example—were all unrehearsed, spontaneous comments from average people on the street (the exception was a well-spoken pastor leading a group to the Holy Land).

A taxi driver mistaken about an archaeological detail proves nothing about Christianity—only that he doesn't know much about archaeology.

Personally, I wouldn't go to a taxi driver to learn about archaeology any more than I would go to a Bible scholar for directions if I were lost. The scholar may want to be helpful, but when I'm lost, I'm going to listen to the taxi driver. The fact that a Christian taxi driver may be mistaken about an archaeological detail doesn't disprove Christianity. It only proves he doesn't know much about archaeology.

What about the differences among the four Gospel stories? Which would cast greater doubt: that the four accounts had differences, or that the accounts were exactly the same? If all four Gospel accounts recorded the same events in the same way, the scholars who now charge that the differences prove they are *fabrications* would no doubt then complain that the similarities prove they are *plagiaries*.

> *It's intellectually dishonest to decide what you want to prove and then only look for evidence to support your position.*

Doesn't it seem a bit ludicrous to postulate that since the Last Supper is not included in the Gospel of John, the writers of Matthew, Mark, and Luke fabricated the event? It seems much more satisfying to say simply, "John did not include the Last Supper in his Gospel, and he had a very good reason for not doing so." There are differences because each writer had a different purpose and different audiences. The essential facts are true and rock-solid.

When does a scholar cease to be a scholar? A scholar is no longer a scholar when he or she allows personal belief or unbelief to predetermine his or her conclusions. It is intellectually dishonest to decide what you want to prove and then only look for evidence to support the position you have already taken.

Is there anything good about these "exposés of Jesus"? It is incredibly interesting that, in spite of these scholars' obvious desire to explain away the deity of Jesus, and as theologically liberal as they are, as a matter of intellectual integrity even they cannot explain away the resurrection. Many of these scholars won't go so far as to say they believe, but they will admit, "Something happened."

Why do they say that? Because if not, it would be the only time in history that a conspiracy of that type had ever held together. Also, if deceivers had intended to devise a false religion, they would not have made up such incredible claims as the Resurrection, the deity of a man, and the working of so many miracles. Nor would they have told so much about their own failures, like deserting Jesus in the face of his terrible suffering. Nor would eleven of the twelve disciples have gone to their deaths for a conspiracy. That theory doesn't work, even for a nonbeliever.

The Uniqueness of the Bible

No higher words have ever been spoken than words from Shakespeare's *Hamlet* that I mentioned in an earlier chapter: "This above all: to thine own self be true, and it must follow as the night the day, thou canst not then be false to any man."

But nowhere in Shakespeare or Aristotle or anywhere else do we find anything comparable to the words of the Bible:

> "For God so loved the world that he gave his one and only Son." (Jesus, John 3:16)

> The Son is the radiance of God's glory and the exact representation of his being, sustaining all things by his powerful word. (Hebrews 1:3)

> "Anyone who has seen me has seen the Father." (Jesus, John 14:9)

"I give them eternal life, and they
shall never perish; no one can
snatch them out of my hand."
(Jesus, John 10:28)

"Friend, your sins are forgiven."
(Jesus, Luke 5:20)

"Lord, to whom shall we go? You
have the words of eternal life."
(Peter, John 6:68)

No one has ever dared to say any words
that even remotely resemble the Bible,
making it the most unique book ever written
by an exponential factor, "the very words of
God."

The Truth of the Bible

The Bible is the "source code" for all things
Christian. Everything
we know about
Christianity comes
from the Bible.

*Exactly what God
wanted to say exactly
the way He wanted to
say it.*

Even a casual
observer of
Christianity knows
there is a huge debate about the truth and
authority of the Bible. Why is the Bible such
a lightning rod? The Bible attracts so much

controversy precisely because it does claim to be the word of God. For example, the Bible contains the following verses:

> "Your word is truth." (Jesus, John 17:17)

> Every word of God is flawless.... (Proverbs 30:5)

> All Scripture is God-breathed and is useful for teaching, rebuking, correcting and training in righteousness. (2 Timothy 3:16)

> For everything that was written in the past was written to teach us, so that...we might have hope. (Romans 15:4)

The Bible claims to be a flawless record of exactly what God wanted to say exactly the way He wanted to say it.

While an internal claim cannot prove that the Bible is the Word of God, it is a staggering claim, and of priceless value if true. Of course, if the Bible did not make this claim, there would be no

What cannot be known about God and redemption through nature is revealed through the written word.

debate. But since it does, and since millions of Christians through the ages have believed the Scriptures are true, it is a question every thinking person must settle in his or her own mind: Is the Bible true?

The historic Christian view is that God-inspired human writers with His very thoughts, which they expressed through their own personalities. Christianity teaches that the Bible is true and without error.

Christianity is a "revealed" religion. In Chapter 5 we saw how God reveals himself in nature, and that the idea of God is an intuition we know is true. Christians call that *general revelation.*

The Bible is *special revelation,* which simply means that what cannot be known about God and redemption through nature is revealed through the written word. The Bible is so important because it claims to be the map by which we understand the life and work of Jesus, the way to salvation ("the gospel"), and the way to godly living ("the teachings").

Tying It All Together

One day I went to a favorite garden center to purchase some spring annuals. It was a warm day and, noticing my warm-up suit, Amy, the twenty-five-year-old woman who waited on me, struck up a conversation. "I'll bet you're hot in that outfit," she said.

"Well, it is a little warm," I said. "How about you? You work in this heat all day."

"You don't know the half of it," she began. "I just moved back from Vermont, and I'm having a tough time adjusting to the Florida heat."

"Oh," I said, "what were you doing in Vermont?"

"Well, I had to get away to try and find myself," she offered.

"So how did you do?" I asked.

"Well, to tell you the truth, I'm pretty confused. My father is from India, my mother is a nominal Catholic, and my brother is a Baptist who keeps wagging his finger in my face and yelling that if I don't accept Jesus, I'm going to hell. I've been studying world religions, and I think there are many ways to God. What do you think?"

"Actually, you're probably asking the wrong person," I said. "You see, I'm what you might call a born-again Christian. In other words, I have put my faith in Jesus Christ to forgive my sins and give me eternal life. But it does bother me that your brother would confront you like that. I guess that's not a very sensitive way of making his point, is it?"

"No," she said, "it's not."

"Listen, Amy," I continued. "Your brother is basically talking like a nut. Even if he's right, that's no way to talk about matters of faith. Let me suggest something for you to consider.

"If you go to the tomb of Confucius—occupied. If you go to the tomb of Buddha—occupied. If you go to the tomb of Mohammed—occupied. If you go to the tomb of Jesus—empty. That intrigues me, Amy, and it ought to intrigue you, too.

"Wow. That's heavy," said Amy.

"Yes, it is. And I think you owe it to yourself to investigate that issue. Jesus is the only one of those four men who claimed to be God. If that's true, then don't you think you owe it to yourself to find out if He really is who He says He is?"

"Yeah, but there's no way to know for sure," she offered lamely.

"Actually, there is," I suggested. "Do you have a Bible?"

"Oh, yes," she said. "My brother gave me a big, thick Life Application Bible."

"Okay, then. Let me make a suggestion. Is that all right?" She nodded approval. "In the Bible, there's a short book called the Gospel of John. It contains twenty-one chapters. Why don't you investigate the claims of Jesus for yourself—who He claimed to be, why He came to earth, and what belief in Him means? You could read a chapter a day for three weeks.

"John recorded some of Jesus' most remarkable words in those few pages. I would also suggest you begin each time by praying something like, 'Jesus, if you are God, then I'm asking you to reveal yourself to me in these pages.' Frankly, Amy, I can't do any better than that. If He is who He says He is, then He doesn't need me to argue His case. You can decide for yourself. What do you think?"

"You know, I think I'll do that," she said conclusively.

The Bible is about Jesus Christ. Jesus said, "You diligently study the Scriptures because you think that by them you possess eternal life. These are the Scriptures that testify about me" (John 5:39).

The "Scriptures" Jesus referred to are what we now call the Old Testament—the Scriptures of His day. The New Testament is all about Jesus as well.

Deciding for Yourself

You can decide for yourself whether or not to believe the Bible is true, and whether you can stake your life on it. You could do this by reading it for yourself. Perhaps you'd want to follow the suggestion I made to Amy—reading the Gospel of John, a chapter a day for three weeks. Interact with the text, asking questions like:

Why did the writer record these particular sayings and events?

What was his purpose for writing his book?

What is being said?

Does what is being said make sense?

What does Jesus say?

What does Jesus do?

Why does Jesus say and do these things?

How did the people respond?

How do I respond?

What does Jesus claim about Himself?

What does Jesus claim about believing in Him?

Does this book hang together?

Does this book have the ring of authority?

Does this book make sense?
Does this book have the ring of truth to me personally?

You don't have to trick yourself into Christianity. Let Jesus speak for Himself. Once you have come to understand, if Jesus doesn't draw you, nothing this or any other book can add will draw you either.

Part Three:

Making Christianity Your Own

Chapter 9

How to Become a Christian

Would you like to become a Christian? Or, if you have previously received Jesus but, for whatever reasons, have not been walking with Him, would you like to reaffirm your faith?

If so, how can you do that?

It's As Simple As a Story

Becoming a Christian is about making a change, but it's not a change that takes place by someone like me telling you how you should live. Likewise, it's not a change you can make by willing yourself to be "good." We've all tried that and failed, haven't we?

> *Becoming a Christian is about embracing the story of Jesus.*

Instead, becoming a Christian is about understanding and embracing the story of Jesus—who He is, why He came, and what it means to believe in Him. Noted theologian J. Gresham Machen put it this way:

The strange thing about Christianity was that it adopted an entirely different method. It transformed the lives of men not by appealing to the human will, but by telling a story; not by exhortation, but by the narration of an event.

It is no wonder that such a method seemed strange. Could anything be more impractical than the attempt to influence conduct by rehearsing events concerning the death of a religious teacher?...

But the strange thing is that it works.... Where the most eloquent exhortation fails, the simple story of an event succeeds; the lives of men are transformed by a piece of news.[29]

Let's review this "simple story," but first let's put the story in perspective.

29. J. Gresham Machen, *Christianity and Liberalism* (Grand Rapids: Wm. B. Eerdmans Publishing Company, 1932), 47-48.

Putting the Story of Jesus in Perspective

According to the Bible, God loves you very much. "How great is the love the Father has lavished on us, that we should be called children of God! And that is what we are!" (1 John 3:1).

You are created in the image of God. "So God created man in his own image, in the image of God he created him; male and female he created them" (Genesis 1:27).

Though created for glory and honor, we have all sinned and gone astray. "For all have sinned and fall short of the glory of God" (Romans 3:23). We are not righteous people who occasionally sin. Confusion here leads to confusion everywhere. We are sinners who stand guilty before a holy and perfect God.

Nevertheless, because of His love for you, God wants you to be saved. "God our Savior…wants all people to be saved and to come to a knowledge of the truth" (1 Timothy 2:3-4). "He is patient with you, not wanting anyone to perish, but everyone to come to repentance" (2 Peter 3:9).

God wants to reconcile His relationship with you. "All this is from God, who reconciled us to himself through Christ and gave us the ministry of reconciliation: that God was reconciling the world to himself in

Christ, not counting men's sins against them" (2 Corinthians 5:18-19).

How does this salvation and reconciliation take place?

The Story of Jesus

Jesus Christ is how God saves sinners and brings them to eternal life. "Here is a trustworthy saying that deserves full acceptance: Christ Jesus came into the world to save sinners" (1 Timothy 1:15). "This is how God showed his love among us: He sent his one and only Son into the world that we might live through him" (1 John 4:9). "For God so loved the world that he gave his one and only Son, that whoever believes in him shall not perish but have eternal life" (John 3:16).

> *Jesus Christ is how God saves sinners and brings them to eternal life.*

Jesus is God. Jesus said, "Anyone who has seen me has seen the Father" (John 14:9 NLT), and also, "The Father and I are one" (John 10:30 NLT). Elsewhere, the Bible declares, "For in Christ all the fullness of the Deity lives in bodily form" (Colossians 2:9). "Christ is the visible image of the invisible God" (Colossians 1:15 NLT). And, "The Son is the radiance of God's glory

and the exact representation of his being"
(Hebrews 1:3).

Jesus loves you very much. He said, "As
the Father has loved me, so have I loved
you" (John 15:9). He has compassion for you.
"When he [Jesus] saw the crowds, he had
compassion on them, because they were
harassed and helpless, like sheep without a
shepherd" (Matthew 9:36).

Jesus came to give you an abundant life,
not evil and futility. "The thief comes only to
steal and kill and destroy; I have come that
they may have life, and have it to the full"
(John 10:10).

Even though He himself lived a sinless
life, because of God's great love for you,
Jesus Christ died for your sins. "But God
showed his great love for us by sending
Christ to die for us while we were still sinners" (Romans 5:8 NLT). "God made him who
had no sin to be sin for us, so that in him we
might become the righteousness of God"
(2 Corinthians 5:21).

After His death, Jesus was raised from the
dead. The apostle Paul said:

> For what I received I passed on
> to you as of first importance: that
> Christ died for our sins accord-
> ing to the Scriptures, that he was
> buried, that he was raised on

the third day according to the
Scriptures, and that he appeared
to Peter, and then to the Twelve.
After that, he appeared to more
than five hundred of the brothers
at the same time. (1 Corinthians
15:3-6)

Through His life, death, and resurrection,
Jesus made an atoning sacrifice for your
sins. "Atoning" means that if you believe in
Him, He has actually taken the punishment
you deserved when He died on the cross.
"He is the atoning sacrifice for our sins, and
not only for ours but also for the sins of the
whole world" (1 John 2:2). "This is love: not
that we loved God, but that he loved us and
sent his Son as an atoning sacrifice for our
sins" (1 John 4:10).

There is no other Savior. Jesus Himself
said, "I am the way and the truth and the life.
No one comes to the Father except through
me" (John 14:6). "Salvation is found in no one
else, for there is no other name under heaven
given to men by which we must be saved"
(Acts 4:12).

To summarize, Jesus, the Son of God, con-
ceived by the Holy Spirit, became a man,
lived a sinless life, was crucified as a sacrifice
for the sins of all men, was buried, was resurrected to life, ascended to heaven where

He lives today with God the Father, and will come again to redeem those who believe in Him.

How We Receive Salvation

We are saved by grace through faith. "For it is by grace you have been saved, through faith—and this is not from yourselves, it is the gift of God—not by works, so that on one can boast" (Ephesians 2:8-9). God changes our minds and hearts by His grace.

> *Jesus is your Savior and Lord. He died for your sins. Through faith your sins are forgiven.*

We must personally believe in and accept Jesus. "But to all who believed him and accepted him, he gave the right to become children of God" (John 1:12 NLT). "If anyone acknowledges that Jesus is the Son of God, God lives in him and he in God" (1 John 4:15).

We must personally acknowledge that we are sinners who need a Savior and Lord. "If we claim to be without sin, we deceive our-selves and the truth is not in us. If we confess our sins, he is faithful and just and will forgive us our sins and purify us from all unright-eousness" (1 John 1:8-9).

Becoming a Christian means believing that Jesus is your Savior and Lord, that He died for your sins, and that through faith your sins are forgiven. In other words, "If you confess with your mouth that Jesus is Lord and believe in your heart that God raised him from the dead, you will be saved" (Romans 10:9 NLT).

You can become a Christian by making a decision (as an act of your will) that, based on the evidence, you are convinced beyond a reasonable doubt, and you believe Jesus loves you and died on the cross for your sins. If so, you can ask Jesus to come into your life, forgive your sins, give you the gift of eternal life, and begin the great adventure for which you were created.

Let's suppose that you believe—or want to believe—but you still have lingering concerns. What should you do about them? Let's look at a few examples.

Dealing with Regrets, Doubts, and Uncertainty

"But I have regrets, feel unworthy, and still have doubts," you say. That's okay. You don't need to pretend you don't have doubts. Doubts are normal. There was a man in the Bible who said to Jesus, "I do believe; help me overcome my unbelief!" (Mark 9:24). And

Jesus did help him. Faith need not be big to get started. It can be small, like a mustard seed. It will grow over time. Cru founder, Bill Bright, often said, "Faith is like a muscle. The more you use it, the bigger it gets."

> *Doubts are normal.*

You might say, "But I did give Christianity a try and it didn't take." Often, people try to follow a God of their own design. But you can't put conditions on God, such as, "I'll believe if you save my marriage." Nor can you expect something in return, such as, "I will believe if God will bless me financially." And you can't give God less than first place, such as, "I will make time for God as soon as I build my career." These are not examples of "giving Christianity a try and it not taking." These are examples of trying something else. Professor and author Ron Nash said, "I have no problem if people want to make up a new religion. I just wish they wouldn't call it Christianity." Christianity can't be what you want it to be; it has to be what it is.

Maybe you've said, "I did try, and it was too hard." You may have been told, "Just pray this prayer and God will bless you." God *will* bless you, but whoever told you that left out hard things like repentance, good deeds, and even suffering. The apostle Paul said, "I preached that they should repent and turn to God and prove their repentance by their deeds" (Acts 26:20). The apostle Peter noted, "Dear friends, do not be surprised at the painful trial you are suffering, as though something strange were happening to you. But rejoice that you participate in the sufferings of Christ, so that you may be overjoyed when his glory is revealed" (1 Peter 4:12-13). As English writer G. K. Chesterton said, "Christianity has not so much been tried and found wanting, as it has been found difficult and left untried."

Or you said, "It's too late for me. I had my chance." It's never too late. God loves you very much. No matter what you've done, you can be forgiven. Jesus told a parable about this in Matthew 20. A man hired people throughout the day to work in his field. At the end of the day, those who only worked a short time were paid the same as those who had worked all day. The reward is the same for all who decide to follow Christ, no matter how late you start following Him.

Giving Christianity a Try

Would it make sense for your daughter to say, "I could never ride a bike," when she had never given it a try?

Or, suppose a boy at a school party wanted to ask a girl to dance. But he didn't ask because he thought, *She would never want to dance with me.* Would it be right for him to now dislike her for not doing what he never asked?

> *It doesn't make sense to reject something you've never tried.*

Or, if a doctor prescribed a medicine for your illness and you didn't take it, would be fair to say, "That medicine doesn't work"?

Or, should someone who refuses to ask for directions be irritated with the mapmaker when they arrive at the wrong destination?

It just doesn't make sense to reject something you've never tried. In the same way it wouldn't be fair to reject Christianity because you never tried it.

So are you ready to give it a try?

How to Become a Christian

You can become a Christian right now.

There is no "standard" way to receive, or renew, salvation. You could be weepy with the salty taste of repentant tears running down your face. You could just as easily feel reserved, cerebral, and scientific. Your experience could range from the blinding light of a

"Damascus road" to "the still small voice of God."

You only need to go as far as you can comprehend. Bishop William Temple said, "Conversion is simply to give as much of yourself as you can to as much of God as you can understand."

> *If you let Jesus in, He will start changing your life.*

If you are ready to receive or come back to Christ, all you have to do is tell Him, simply, in your own words:

That your heart is restless and you need God

That you are truly sorry for your sins

That you know you need a Savior

That you put your faith in Jesus

That you humbly and gratefully receive His love and forgiveness

That you humbly and gratefully accept His salvation and eternal life

That you want Him to transform you into a disciple who leads a

powerful life in right relationship
with God and right relationship
with others.

You can do this silently or out loud. If you
don't know exactly how to put it, you can
pray the following prayer (or one similar to it):

Lord Jesus, my heart is restless,
and I need You. I am filled with a
deep sorrow for my sins. I ask for
Your forgiveness. I believe in You,
Jesus. I believe You came and
died for my sins. By grace through
faith, I receive You as my Savior
and Lord. Thank You for Your forgiveness, for giving me the gift of
eternal life, and for the promise of
an abundant life. Please change
me from the inside out. Amen.

Take a moment to pray this prayer and
let Jesus in. If you do, He will start changing
your life. It's what you do next that counts.

If you prayed and received Christ, or reaf-
firmed your faith in Him, welcome to the
family, or welcome back. The next chapter will suggest a few steps you can take to
develop a deepening relationship with Him.

Chapter 10
How to Have a Deepening Relationship With God

Becoming a Christian is both an "act" and a "process."

The "act" of becoming a Christian is called *justification*. It's like getting your driver's license—now you're legal. It's happens at a moment in time when, as discussed in the last chapter, you act upon the gospel message. As the apostle Paul said, "Therefore, since we have been justified through faith, we have peace with God through our Lord Jesus Christ" (Romans 5:1).

Christianity teaches that once you have truly been *justified*—that is, declared righteous before God—you will be a Christian always and forever. You can never lose the salvation God grants. Jesus said it this way:

> My sheep listen to my voice; I
> know them, and they follow me.
> I give them eternal life, and they
> shall never perish; *no one can
> snatch them out of my hand*. My
> Father, who has given them to

me, is greater than all; *no one can snatch them out of my Father's hand*. (John 10:27-29, emphasis added)

The "process" of becoming a Christian is called *sanctification*. Christianity also teaches that God will *sanctify* you, or make you holy, but you must also seek holiness, which simply means, to become more like Christ. "It is God's will that you should be sanctified" (1 Thessalonians 4:3).

As the saying goes, God loves you just the way you are, but He loves you too much to leave you that way.

I mentioned that you don't need to know how an engine works in order to drive a car. You do, however, need to know a few things about driving. Embracing "the gospel" is like getting your driver's license, "the teachings" make it safe for you to be on the road.

Gratitude, not duty, motivates Christians to obey the Bible.

"The teachings" in the Bible tell us how to imitate Christ; it is a system—a worldview. Christian philosopher Francis Schaeffer once observed that after someone becomes a Christian, we have a responsibility to help him or her gain a biblical worldview. If we don't, said Schaeffer, we risk losing them to an alien worldview—basically back to a secular, moral, or religious worldview.

It is not *duty* that motivates Christians to obey the teachings, but *gratitude*—a gratitude that grows as the believer increasingly understands the grace that has been freely given. "Now I commit you to God and to the word of his grace, which can build you up and give you an inheritance among all those who are sanctified" (Acts 20:32).

Heart Transformation

The core value of all religious belief systems *except* Christianity is behavior modification and performance— combinations of strict religious observances, legalism, animal sacrifices, worship of multiple gods, asceti-

> *Christianity is not about behavior modification; it's about heart transformation.*

cism, self-denial, religious exclusion of certain classes, harsh treatment of women, and even violence against defecting members.

After I became a Christian, I assumed the core value of Christianity, like the religions I had known, was behavior modification and performance—to "act Christianly"—a view I mistakenly held for fourteen years. I knew I was saved by grace, but I figured it was up to me to prove that God had not made a mistake!

Exactly *not* that. Christianity is not *behavior modification* (a thing I do) but *heart transformation* (a thing grace does). Romans 12:2 teaches, "Don't copy the behavior and customs of this world, *but let God transform you into a new person by changing the way you think*" (NLT, emphasis added).

Notice that this text does *not* say, "Don't copy the behavior and customs of this world, *but copy the behavior and customs of Christ.*" That would simply be substituting a system that doesn't work with a system we can't keep. It would be using human strength, desire, discipline, and will to modify our behavior and perform—a tiring game you can play well for no more than a few hours at a time.

Instead, the essence of what Romans 12:2 teaches is that Christianity is not what you do for God by intense human effort, but what God does for you by sheer grace. Romans 9:16 puts it this way: "It does not, therefore, depend on man's desire or effort, but on God's mercy."

The core value of the Christian system is heart transformation. We certainly put in effort. But we don't change ourselves; we let

God change the way we think. Philippians 2:12-13 perfectly explains the relationship between our effort and God's work:

> Therefore, my dear friends, as you have always obeyed—not only in my presence, but now much more in my absence—continue to work out your salvation with fear and trembling, for it is God who works in you to will and to act according to his good purpose.

Behavior *does* become modified, but it is because God works in us to sanctify us, giving us the desire to obey Him and the power to do what pleases Him. "May God himself, the God of peace, sanctify you through and through. May your whole spirit, soul and body be kept blameless at the coming of our Lord Jesus Christ" (1 Thessalonians 5:23).

Here are a handful of practical ideas to help you grow in your faith.

1. Make Jesus the Lord of Your Life

Consider Jeff. He believed that Jesus Christ was his Savior. Like so many of us, he assumed it was up to him to live in a way that was worthy of the name "Christian." His experience, however, was that he couldn't. He wondered why his life was so powerless— until he attended a college campus-ministry meeting where, he said, "I heard that Christ is the Lord of our lives."

Some people know Christ as Lord and don't live accordingly, but others just don't know. Jeff simply didn't know. The right kind of teaching can change everything.

What does it mean to make Jesus the Lord of your life? It means choosing to follow Him and His teaching. To put aside your own best thinking when you realize it contradicts the Bible. To live for God's approval rather than another person's or even your own. "But in your hearts set apart Christ as Lord" (1 Peter 3:15).

> *The right kind of teaching can change everything.*

2. Spend Time With God

One thing inexperienced Christians some-times find irritating about experienced Christians is their relentless talk about "spending time with God." A rabid Republican will, of course, irritate even a mild Democrat, and an enthusiastic football fan will unnerve almost anyone pulling for the other team, but why do people on the same team see things differently?

A friend of mine, John Smith, says, "If someone told you that if you spent thirty minutes a day with a person for one year, then you would receive $10,000,000, it's pretty certain you would do whatever it takes to have that $10,000,000." Experienced Christians are so relentless about "spending time with God" because they actually believe they have found something so valuable that they willingly forsake (that is, make secondary) all things to possess it.

In the same way, once you embrace Christ, you too will find a growing desire—perhaps an ache—to know more about the Sustainer and Redeemer of your soul. It has been well said that, "The soul that has once been waked, or stung, or uplifted by the desire for God, will inevitably awake to the fear of losing him."[30]

Try the "crawl, walk, run" approach. If you're just getting started, consider spending a few minutes at least four days a week reading and meditating on the Bible. Perhaps read a chapter

> *Happiness is the residue of holiness.*

---

30. C. S. Lewis, *Letters to Malcolm, Chiefly on Prayer,* 1964, New York: Harcourt, Inc., 76.

in the New Testament and say the Lord's
Prayer. That should take about five minutes.
When you're appetite increases, try a one-
year Bible reading plan (search for "Bible
reading plans" online) or buy *The One Year
Bible.*

When you read, remember that it's part
of God's "process" of sanctification: "All
Scripture is God-breathed and is useful for
teaching, rebuking, correcting and train-
ing in righteousness, so that the man of God
may be thoroughly equipped for every good
work" (2 Timothy 3:16-17).

The Bible will interpret very differently if
you're reading it for happiness rather than
for holiness. We don't become sanctified by
seeking happiness. Instead, happiness is the
residue of holiness.

3. Expect Spiritual Warfare

If God created and saved us, why do we continue to sin? We are a product of both the
Creation and the Fall. The Creation made us
in the image of God; the Fall made us like a
devil.

The Bible teaches that we will always
struggle against sin on this side of heaven
because of the influence of the world, our
sinful natures, and the devil. But we can

increasingly have victory by putting on the armor of God—truth, righteousness, the gospel, faith, the word of God, the Holy Spirit, and prayer.

Here's how the Bible puts it:

> Finally, be strong in the Lord and in his mighty power. Put on the full armor of God so that you can take your stand against the devil's schemes. For our struggle is not against flesh and blood, but against the rulers, against the authorities, against the powers of this dark world and against the spiritual forces of evil in the heavenly realms.
>
> Therefore put on the full armor of God, so that when the day of evil comes, you may be able to stand your ground, and after you have done everything, to stand. Stand firm then, with the belt of truth buckled around your waist, with the breastplate of righteousness in place, and with your feet fitted with the readiness that comes from the gospel of peace.
>
> In addition to all this, take up the shield of faith, with which you can extinguish all the flaming

arrows of the evil one. Take the helmet of salvation and the sword of the Spirit, which is the word of God. And pray in the Spirit on all occasions with all kinds of prayers and requests. With this in mind, be alert and always keep on praying for all the saints. (Ephesians 6:10-18)

4. Embrace the Principles of a Sanctified Life

Many books have been written to help us in the sanctification process, but here are a few basics about the principles of a sanctified life, and a declaration that you can make about each if you want.

> God: I will seek to love God with all my heart, root out anything that distracts me from Him, and all that this implies.

> Personal Holiness: I will seek to lead a holy life, and all that this implies.

> Marriage: I will seek to be a faithful, loving spouse (if applicable), and all that this implies.

Children: I will seek to be a godly parent and grandparent (if applicable), and all that this implies.

Friendship: I will seek to be a loving, honest friend, and all that this implies.

Work: I will seek to honor God in my work, and all that this implies.

Ministry: I will seek to serve God by building His kingdom, and all that this implies.

Money: I will seek to be a faithful steward, and all that this implies.

Health: I will seek to lead a balanced life, and all that this implies.

Church: I will seek to join and support a church community, and all that this implies.

Integrity: I will seek to lead a life above reproach, and all that this implies.

It would be easy to convert these declarations into a "To-Do list" in order to earn favor or merit with God—it happens all the time.

That would simply be inserting Christian values into a moral or religious system. Do the right thing, but *not* for the wrong reason. The right reason is because you are grateful to God for salvation.

5. Join a Small Group Bible Study Through a Local Church

Someone once asked the famous evangelist Billy Graham, "If you were a pastor of a large church in a principal city, what would be your plan of action?"

I would have imagined that Rev. Graham would outline a mass evangelistic plan to take the city by storm. Instead, in *The Master Plan of Evangelism,* it's reported that he answered, "One of the first things I would do would be to get a small group of eight or ten or twelve men around me that would meet a few hours a week and pay the price! It would cost them something in time and effort. I would share with them everything I have, over a period of years. Then I would actually have twelve ministers...who in turn could take eight or ten or twelve more and teach them."[31] Not a bad idea. It has been done before with some success (smile).

31. Robert E. Coleman, *The Master Plan of Evangelism* (Old Tappan: Fleming H Revell Company, 1963), 120.

Personally, I have never known anyone whose life has changed in any significant way apart from the regular study of God's Word. We can do nothing more concrete to get to know God than to study the Bible.

Most people do not have the aptitude, interest, or time to do the close work to study Bible passages in depth. That's why it's valuable to attend a Bible study in which a teacher takes Scripture, helps you discover what it means, and shows how you can apply it to your life.

You may have received this book at a church. That church would be a good place to pursue a Bible study. Ask for help. You could attend a couples' study, a men's group, or a women's study. If you're married and it's possible, attend with your spouse.

6. Walk in the Spirit

No one, of course, can do all these things. We are human beings, not machines. For that reason the Holy Spirit offers us ongoing power to obey, and Jesus offers us ongoing forgiveness when we don't. "But the Counselor, the Holy Spirit, whom the Father will send in my name, will teach you all things and will remind you of everything I have said to you" (John 14:26).

Our calling is to live by the Spirit, not the flesh. But when we sin, which we will continue to do, we must confess it, accept God's ongoing forgiveness, and invite the Spirit of Christ to guide us. The Bible says, "But when he, the Spirit of truth, comes, he will guide you into all truth" (John 16:13). And when we fail, Hebrews 5:2 teaches that "[Jesus] is able to deal gently with those who are ignorant and are going astray."

There's a wonderful story that illustrates how the Holy Spirit transforms us to become like Jesus. An elementary school class went to the studio of a famous sculptor. As the children entered, they had to pass by the statue of a very ferocious and realistic lion.

One of the students said, "Hey mister, how were you able to make such a realistic looking lion?"

He answered, "Son, it was easy. I took a large block of marble, and then I simply chipped away everything that didn't look like a lion."

In the same way, think of yourself as a large block of marble. Present yourself to God every day, and invite the Holy Spirit to chip away everything that doesn't look like Jesus.

Afterword

As you have been able to see for yourself, it is not unreasonable to believe that Christianity is true.

What makes Christianity so encouraging is that it provides meaningful answers to our deepest questions—questions for which other belief systems simply don't have satisfying answers. There are agreeable explanations to resolve our doubts. God wants to redeem our lives from futility, despair, sin, and death. We are not alone. Someone cares. God cares. And that's an idea that is overwhelming.

As you now turn your attention back to your everyday life, let me encourage you to do two things. First, take Jesus Christ with you. Let Him transform your heart. Say grace over everything, not just meals. Invite the Lord to be part of every detail of your life. Second, think of someone who needs to read this book and give it to them.

Keep the faith. I've been praying for you.

—*Patrick Morley, Winter Park, Florida*

Acknowledgments

Much of this book was adapted from a larger work entitled, *Coming Back to God*. I would especially like to thank Brett Clemmer for championing the idea to take that book and compress it into this smaller, more focused volume.

Also, special thanks to David Delk and Brett Clemmer for their unflinching courage to make the tough and wise edits needed to make this book the best it could be for you, my reader, as well as Corrie Cochran, for gracefully coordinating the publishing process.

Thanks also to Jamie Turco and Lauren Simonic for their diligent proofreading, Cathleen Kwas for her engaging layout and typesetting, and Kevin McMillan for his outstanding cover design. It's an honor to work with such talented people.

I owe a special debt of gratitude to Dr. Charles MacKenzie for teaching me about the relationship between theology and science.

Thanks to my colleagues at Man in the Mirror for making it possible for me to pursue my love for writing: Al Lenio, Bill Chapman, Brett Clemmer, Brian Russell, Carol Hetrick, Christina Angelakos, Corrie Cochran, Dave Hamilton, David Delk, Jeff Kisiah, Jamie Turco, Kimberly Massari, Laraine Irvin, Lucy Blair, Roddey Roberts, Ruth Cameron, Scott Russell, Sharon Carey, Tom Hingle, Tracie Searles, Jim Seibert and all of our Area Directors.

And also to our Board of Directors: Dr. Pete Alwinson, Bill Helms, Sidney Hinton, Fred Mateer, Larry Mattingly, Jimmy Pendley, and Todd Woodard, Sr. Thank you so much for making it possible for me to write.

man in the mirror
For every church to disciple every man

Man in the Mirror believes that Christ has called His church to reach men and help them lead powerful, transformed lives. Since 1986, Man in the Mirror has worked with more than 25,000 churches and millions of men. We help churches reach and disciple men with three interlocking strategies:

Leadership Training with No Man Left Behind

Churches that implement the No Man Left Behind Model report a 48% increase in the number of men attending, and an 84% increase in participation in men's discipleship—in just 2 ½ years! We train leaders to cast vision, assess the spiritual state of their men, and develop an intentional plan to disciple all their men. Learn more at **maninthemirror.org/nmlbmodel**.

Men's Discipleship with the Journey to Biblical Manhood

The Journey to Biblical Manhood is a flexible process that provides churches with 12 Challenges, fully customizable with templates and timelines to disciple men in the major areas of the Christian life. Learn more at **journeytobiblicalmanhood.org**.

Local Coaching with Area Directors

Area Directors link arms with pastors and leaders in their area to help them disciple men. They serve as local men's discipleship experts to any church that wants help. They also coordinate a local Coalition for Men's Discipleship, made up of churches and leaders committed to the cause. Learn more at **areadirectors.org**.

www.maninthemirror.org

Equipped for Life

Finally, a men's devotional magazine for men who are willing to dream big, think big, and risk big.

You've never read anything like this. Short devotions written just for men, applying Biblical truth to topics men face every day. Plus, questions to help you go deeper and articles to help you grow and lead others. All in a quarterly magazine that's easy to read and easy to share.

Subscribe today at
www.maninthemirror.org.

You Don't Have to Settle

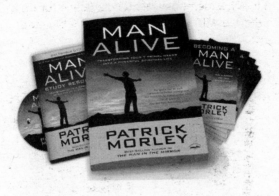

Transform the raw, restless energy you feel into a passionate devotion to Christ. The collection of Man Alive resources is great for individual or small group study.

Look for a special edition of the Man Alive enhanced eBook.

Also Available as an eBook

Visit www.ManAliveBook.com to watch the video and read an excerpt.

MAKE YOUR COLOR SELECTIONS BEFORE READING THE TEXT OF THIS BOOK

PRELIMINARY INSTRUCTIONS FOR CONDUCTING THE COLOR TEST

1. Remove the eight color cards from the insert between pages 92 and 93. Shuffle them and lay them out—color side up—in front of you.

2. Look the eight colors over and decide which color you like best. *DO NOT try to associate the color with something else,* such as dress materials, furnishings, automobiles, etc. Just choose the color for which you feel the most sympathy out of the eight colors in front of you.

3. Pick the chosen card and place it—color side down —above and to the left of the remaining seven.

4. Look at the remaining colors, choose the one which you *now* like best out of those that are visible and place it—color side down—beside and to the right of your previous choice.

5. Repeat number 4 with the remaining colors, one by one, until all eight are in a row, color side down, with the most-liked color on the left and the least-liked color on the right.

6. Read off, from left to right, the numbers appearing on the backs of the cards and write them down in order on a piece of paper.

7. Pick up the eight color cards, re-shuffle them, and lay them out again—color side up—in front of you.

I

8. Repeat numbers 2 to 6. *DO NOT* consciously try to remember or reproduce your first selection. (Neither should you make a conscious effort *not* to reproduce it.) Just choose the colors as if you were seeing them for the first time.

9. Write down the numbers of the second selection on the same piece of paper as the first, below the numbers already recorded. (Do not lose this piece of paper, as you will need these recorded selections after you have read the text.)

PRELIMINARY INTERPRETATION

1. Having made your two selections, you will have two series of eight numbers one below the other, for example:

$$5 \quad 1 \quad 4 \quad 3 \quad 2 \quad 0 \quad 6 \quad 7$$
$$1 \quad 4 \quad 5 \quad 2 \quad 3 \quad 6 \quad 0 \quad 7$$

2. Divide each row up into pairs, the first pair being marked "+", the second pair "×", the third pair "=", and the fourth pair "−". In the example, this will result in the following groups:

+ 5 + 1	× 4 × 3	= 2 = 0	− 6 − 7
+ 1 + 4	× 5 × 2	= 3 = 6	− 0 − 7

3. Additionally, the first and last figure in each row constitute a fifth group, which is marked "+ −". This gives two more groups:

$$+ 5 - 7 \text{ and } + 1 - 7.$$

4. Turn to Table I of the Interpretation Tables (p. 96) which gives the interpretation of the "+" functions, and read the interpretations for groups + 5 + 1 and + 1 + 4.

II

5. Table II (p. 105) will provide the interpretations for the "×" functions.

Table III (p. 116) gives the interpretations for the "=" functions.

Table IV (p. 126) gives the interpretations for the "−" functions.

Table V (p. 157) gives the interpretations for the "+−" functions.

(NOTE: The second selection usually occurs more spontaneously and is therefore more valid then the first selection, especially in doubtful cases.)

6. Now that your color selections are on record, go ahead and read the text. Then, if you choose, you can re-group and mark your selections as described in Chapters 3 and 4, and make a more comprehensive analysis.

The Lüscher Color Test
was originally published by
Random House, Inc.